Understanding Biblical Evidence

Books in this series

Preparing for a Bahá'í/Christian Dialogue

VOLUME 1

UNDERSTANDING BIBLICAL EVIDENCE

by

Michael W. Sours

ONEWORLD
OXFORD

Preparing for a Bahá'í/Christian Dialogue

Volume 1
Understanding Biblical Evidence

Oneworld Publications Ltd
185 Banbury Road, Oxford, OX2 7AR

© Michael Sours 1990

ISBN 1-85168-018-7

Typeset by Fine Line Publishing Services, Witney
Printed and bound in Great Britain by
Redwood Press Limited, Melksham, Wiltshire

contents

part one

THE BIBLE AND THE BAHÁ'Í FAITH

chapter 1

chapter 2

c h a p t e r   3

c h a p t e r   4

c h a p t e r   5

c h a p t e r   6

p a r t   t w o

UNDERSTANDING   SCRIPTURE

c h a p t e r   7

c h a p t e r   8

p a r t   t h r e e

PROOFS

c h a p t e r   9

c h a p t e r   10

c h a p t e r   11

c h a p t e r 12

p a r t   f o u r

PROGRESSIVE   REVELATION

c h a p t e r 13

c h a p t e r 14

part five

CONCLUSION

chapter   1 5

part   one:

THE BIBLE AND THE BAHÁ'Í FAITH

1

INTRODUCTION

THE PURPOSE OF THIS BOOK

The purpose of this book is to assist Bahá'ís in deepening their understanding of the Bible, and to help those who are interested to prepare themselves for religious discussions with Christians. This book addresses two primary concerns: how to conduct friendly and positive dialogues with Christians, and what information would be the most helpful in such dialogues. Although more pages have been devoted to providing helpful information, without question it is the spirit in which we deliver that information that is the most important factor in our association with followers of other Faiths.

We often find ourselves interacting with Christians in a variety of contexts. For example, we may work with them in community service programs or in our professions, and we may encounter Christians among our family, friends, and neighbors. Such situations provide opportunities for discussing the Bahá'í teachings and explaining why Bahá'ís believe what they believe. However, whatever the circumstances in which we find ourselves discussing the Bahá'í Faith with Christians, we must always keep in mind that Bahá'u'lláh enjoins us to "consort with the followers of all religions in a spirit of friendliness and fellowship" (*Tablets of Bahá'u'lláh 22*).

THREE BASIC PRINCIPLES

Throughout this study we will learn how to apply three important Bahá'í principles that will help us develop and maintain a spirit of friendliness when we discuss the Bahá'í Faith with Christians. These three principles are:

- Emphasizing areas of agreement;
- Listening to other points of view and learning about the scriptures, beliefs, and terminology of those with whom we converse;
- Adapting our presentation to the particular terminology and temperament of the people to whom we speak.

Emphasizing areas of agreement

When we discuss the Bahá'í Faith with Christians, we should seek to emphasize areas of agreement such as shared values, beliefs, and goals, which can form the basis of friendship and mutual respect. It is not difficult to find such areas of agreement since Bahá'ís share many beliefs in common with Christians. For example, the Bahá'í writings clearly state that the divine origin of Christianity is "unconditionally acknowledged, that the Sonship and Divinity of Jesus Christ are fearlessly asserted," and that "the divine inspiration of the Gospel is fully recognized" (Shoghi Effendi, *Promised Day* 109).

When Christians perceive that the Bahá'í Faith has a positive attitude to Christ, the Bible and Christianity, they are more likely to have similar feelings of goodwill toward Bahá'ís. Working to establish such bonds of friendship is extremely important. Bahá'ís are entrusted with the responsibility to be the unifiers of humankind, and all our actions should reflect this spirit. By building unity with others, we demonstrate Bahá'u'lláh's teachings through our actions. Furthermore, such fellowship is an important way for Bahá'ís to gain the support of other groups who are working to advance similar goals such as the establishment of peace, racial justice, and the end of numerous social problems.

As Bahá'ís, we know that we must strive to overcome any prejudices that we may have developed in the course of our lives. Let us pause for a moment and ask ourselves whether we have any prejudices toward Christians. A prejudice is formed when we allow the actions of some Christians to shape our attitude toward other Christians. Perhaps at some time a person identifying himself or herself as a Christian criticized the Bahá'í Faith or caused us some personal harm. Or perhaps we heard about a particular Christian leader who did something inappropriate or a particular group of Christians who promoted a cause or expressed a view that is against Bahá'í teachings, such as racial segregation, sexism, or intolerance of other religions. Whatever the reason, if we carry within us a prejudice, we know as Bahá'ís that we must strive to recognize and overcome it. Furthermore, even when we interact with Christians who are not practicing the teachings of Christ, we should remember Bahá'u'lláh's words, "magnify not the faults of others that thine own faults may not appear great" (*Hidden Words* 37). By overcoming such prejudices and focusing on people's strengths, we will greatly enhance the spirituality of our interactions with Christians.

Listening to Christians and learning their point of view

However, to present the Bahá'í teachings effectively we must learn about Christianity. One of the best ways to gain a knowledge of Christian beliefs is to ask questions and listen to the Christians with whom we associate. The importance and value of listening to others cannot be over-stressed. Many Christians are eager to share their beliefs and will respect the open-mindedness of Bahá'ís. Ask Christians about their beliefs, discuss the Bible, and learn about their concerns. Such discussions can form the basis of firm and lasting friendships. Eventually, opportunities to discuss the Bahá'í teachings will arise. If we allow others to express their views, they are more likely to extend to us the same courtesy. When such opportunities arise, we will be better able to answer Christian questions and explain Bahá'í teachings in an appropriate way. That is, we will if we have taken the time to understand the Christian point of view and have acquired knowledge of their beliefs so that we can speak in a language Christians understand.

Adapting our terminology and presentation to our audience

Much of the terminology in the Bahá'í writings is derived from the Bible, which is part of the religious heritage of the Bahá'í Faith, and thus many Christians will be relatively familiar with it. However, there are some terms and phrases that Bahá'ís use with which Christians are generally not familiar, such as 'progressive revelation,' 'Manifestations,' and 'the World Order of Bahá'u'lláh.' There are also terms that Christians use to explain certain concepts or beliefs with which Bahá'ís may not be familiar, such as 'the rapture,' 'pre-millenialism,' and 'personal relationship with Christ.' We will examine specific examples of terminology later. The reason for mentioning such terms now is to make the point that, because of such differences of terminology, people often misunderstand each other even when they are essentially saying the same thing. In order to avoid such misunderstandings it is best to first familiarize ourselves with Christian beliefs and terms before we try to explain the Bahá'í teachings to Christians. The Bahá'í writings tell us to "mingle with the divers kindreds and peoples of the world; familiarize ourselves with their manners, traditions, thoughts and customs" (Shoghi Effendi, *Bahá'í Administration* 69). Furthermore, the writings say that those who arise to spread Bahá'u'lláh's teachings should not "overlook the fundamental prerequisite for any successful teaching enterprise, which is to adapt the presentation of the fundamental principles of their Faith to the cultural and religious backgrounds, the ideologies, and the temperament of the divers races and nations whom they are called upon to enlighten and attract" (Shoghi Effendi, *Citadel of Faith* 25).

A BRIEF OUTLINE OF THIS MANUAL

Preparing for a Bahá'í/Christian Dialogue is meant to be used as a training manual and study guide. Consequently, it has been written in a simple non-academic way and does not presume or require previous familiarity with the Bible or Christianity. In this volume (Volume One) we will learn about the importance of the Bible, how to study and interpret the Bible, how to use biblical evidence to support the claims of Bahá'u'lláh, and how to present the Bahá'í concept of progressive revelation to Christians.

Many of the issues that are not examined in this book will be presented in Volume Two, which will explore conservative Protestant beliefs about five important Christian doctrines: the inspiration and infallibility of the Bible, the deity of Christ, the Resurrection, the substitutionary atonement, and the Return of Christ. In our study of Christian doctrines, attention will be given to passages in the Bible that Christians have interpreted to form their beliefs, and in some cases we will examine Bahá'í writings which show a remarkable similarity to those verses. By examining the Bible in the light of Bahá'í writings, we will demonstrate the Bible's harmony with Bahá'u'lláh's teachings. Numerous verses from the Bible are examined to provide compelling evidence why Christians should reconsider holding rigidly to certain aspects of their traditional beliefs.

Volume Three is primarily intended as an introduction to prophecy and will help us begin a personal study of biblical prophecy. Why the evidence of prophecy is commonly misunderstood will be explained first. We will analyze the nature and interpretation of prophecies and study ways in which biblical prophecies can assist us in explaining specific aspects of the Bahá'í Faith. We will focus in particular on biblical prophecies that the Bahá'í writings clearly identify with Bahá'u'lláh and, in most cases, both a Bahá'í and a Christian point of view will be presented. We will also learn about biblical prophecies fulfilled by Christ that will enable us to demonstrate that prophecy has a spiritual significance.

When we have reached the final pages of this first volume, we will neither have answered all questions nor covered all issues, and our study of Scripture will have only begun. Nevertheless, we should be better equipped to answer questions without frustration and better able to respond to objections encountered in discussions with Christians. The book aims to promote in its readers a more conscious and spiritual attitude toward how we as Bahá'ís present our ideas and beliefs, an organized and more disciplined approach to the study of Scripture, a deeper appreciation of the Bible and Christianity, a more solid knowledge of the relationship between the Bahá'í Faith and Christianity, and a new level of confidence when talking with Christians.

2

REASONING FROM SCRIPTURE

THE IMPORTANCE OF KNOWING THE BIBLE

Studying the Bible not only increases our knowledge of Christianity it also increases our spiritual understanding of the Bahá'í Faith. In the following reference to the Gospel, Shoghi Effendi suggests the importance of the relationship between the Bible and the Bahá'í Faith:

> From the ... words of Christ, as attested by the Gospel, every unprejudiced observer will readily apprehend the magnitude of the Faith which Bahá'u'lláh has revealed, and recognize the staggering weight of the claim He has advanced. (*World Order* 25)

In as much as Bahá'u'lláh's claims are linked to biblical prophecy, it is not surprising that throughout His writings much of the terminology He uses is rooted in the biblical tradition. These grounds alone provide sufficient reason for Bahá'ís to study the Bible. However, there is another compelling reason, which is the vital prerequisite to know the Bible in order to teach Christians about the Bahá'í Faith.

Some Christians are not moved by reasoning that fails to address teachings found in the Bible. Moreover, for many

Christians the Bible is the sole and final arbiter in settling matters of faith and determining right from wrong, true from false. Hence, knowing only the Bahá'í writings will leave us unprepared to converse effectively with Christians.

In *The Secret of Divine Civilization*, a book addressed to the Muslims of Persia, 'Abdu'l-Bahá explains how important it is to know the Scriptures revered by the one with whom we wish to talk:

> If ... a spiritually learned Muslim is conducting a debate with a Christian and he knows nothing of the glorious melodies of the Gospel, he will, no matter how much he imparts of the Qur'án and its truths, be unable to convince the Christian, and his words will fall on deaf ears. Should, however, the Christian observe that the Muslim is better versed in the fundamentals of Christianity than the Christian priests themselves, and understands the purport of the Scriptures even better than they, he will gladly accept the Muslim's arguments, and he would indeed have no other recourse. (*Secret of Divine Civilization* 36)

When we apply 'Abdu'l-Bahá's point to our situation – a dialogue between Christians and Bahá'ís – the message is clear: if we wish to be persuasive when speaking with Christians, we *must* know the Bible in order to support our claims. Even though one of the most convincing ways to present the truth of the Bahá'í teachings is to show them in practice, not everybody we meet will think good conduct alone is proof of Bahá'u'lláh's claims. We must still try to supplement it with clear and well-reasoned arguments. 'Abdu'l-Bahá emphasizes the significance of this element of teaching:

> If their task is to be confined to good conduct and advice, nothing will be accomplished. They must speak out, expound the proofs, set forth clear arguments, draw

irrefutable conclusions establishing the truth of the manifestation of the Sun of Reality. (*Selections from the Writings of 'Abdu'l-Bahá* 268)

'Abdu'l-Bahá also stresses the importance of using reason and logic in studying religion:

> Consider what it is that singles man out from among created beings, and makes of him a creature apart. Is it not his reasoning power, his intelligence? Shall he not make use of these in his study of religion? I say unto you: weigh carefully in the balance of reason and science everything that is presented to you as religion. If it passes this test, then accept it, for it is truth! If, however, it does not so conform, then reject it, for it is ignorance! (*Paris Talks* 144)

In yet another passage 'Abdu'l-Bahá says:

> You must come into the knowledge of the divine Manifestations and Their teachings through proofs and evidences. (*Promulgation* 227)

In these statements 'Abdu'l-Bahá makes it clear that we should use reason and logic to investigate religious truth. Naturally it follows that when we explain the Bahá'í Faith to others we should present reasonable arguments and evidences in support of the claims of Bahá'u'lláh.

The approach used in *Preparing for a Bahá'í/Christian Dialogue* to help us analyze religious issues rationally consists of three basic steps:

- defining our terminology
- weighing the merits of different types of evidence and
- examining whether the evidence justifies the conclusions.

THE IMPORTANCE OF ADAPTING OUR PRESENTATION TO OUR AUDIENCE

Knowledge of the Bible is not generally sufficient, on its own, for successful and mutually rewarding interchanges with Christians; we also need to learn how best to present the evidence we find in it. Before we attempt to explain the Bahá'í Faith to any group of people, we must be in the proper frame of mind and well prepared. Bahá'u'lláh tells us that our "words and utterances should be both impressive and penetrating. However, no word will be infused with these two qualities unless it be uttered wholly for the sake of God and with due regard unto the exigencies of the occasion and the people" (*Tablets of Bahá'u'lláh* 172). Similarly, Shoghi Effendi counsels us to prepare ourselves by studying the approach best suited to the people we are meeting (*Advent of Divine Justice* 54). For example, it would be very difficult, if not impossible, to persuade a Buddhist by quoting the Bible in support of a Bahá'í argument. Similarly, references to Buddhist Scripture are unlikely to convince Christians.

Reasoning from the Scriptures of the Old Testament is the means by which Christianity itself was originally spread. If we examine the New Testament accounts of early Christians such as Stephen, Apollos, and especially Saint Paul, we find numerous examples of such a method being used. In the Acts of the Apostles, a thirty-year account of the spread of Christianity after Christ's crucifixion, it is recorded that Paul "as his custom was, went in to them, and for three Sabbaths reasoned with them from the Scriptures" (Acts 17:2).

In another chapter of the same book we are given a more detailed description of Paul's approach:

So when they had appointed him [Paul] a day, many came to him at *his* lodging, to whom he explained and solemnly testified of the kingdom of God, persuading them concerning Jesus from both the Law of Moses and the Prophets, from morning till evening. (Acts 28:23)

Reasoning from Scripture is also the method 'Abdu'l-Bahá used in presenting the Bahá'í teachings to His Christian audiences, who were often skeptical about non-scriptural arguments. 'Abdu'l-Bahá presented Bahá'u'lláh's message to Christians by frequently referring to the Bible to support points. That is, He used Scripture as the evidence from which He could draw logical conclusions to support the teachings and claims of Bahá'u'lláh. Thus He used a criterion, the Bible, that both He and His listeners accepted.

'Abdu'l-Bahá's approach can be seen clearly in the talks He gave in Paris and America.[1] For example, in one case He explains the true meaning of religion and the importance of unity, both important Bahá'í principles, by referring to the influence of Christ: "For instance, Christ united various nations, brought peace to warring peoples and established the oneness of humankind" (*Promulgation* 158). In another case 'Abdu'l-Bahá illustrates the equality of men and women, another Bahá'í principle, by referring to the example of Mary Magdalene: "In brief, this woman [Mary Magdalene], singly and alone, was instrumental in transforming the disciples and making them steadfast. This is an evidence of extraordinary power and supreme attributes, a proof that woman is the equivalent and complement of man" (*Promulgation* 395).

Also 'Abdu'l-Bahá uses biblical terms and phrases familiar to His listeners. Some examples include 'sheep,' meaning 'the believers' (*Promulgation* 298); 'Shepherd,' meaning 'the Manifestation' (*Promulgation* 116); 'Father,' meaning 'God' (*Promulgation* 267); and 'fruits,' meaning 'deeds' (*Promulgation* 335–6). In fact, these types of biblical terminology are found in most of the talks 'Abdu'l-Bahá delivered in America.

1. Many of 'Abdu'l-Bahá's talks can be found in *Paris Talks, Promulgation of Universal Peace,* and *'Abdu'l-Bahá in London.*

Over and over, 'Abdu'l-Bahá quotes the Bible to support the Bahá'í teachings; refers frequently to Christ; defends the Christian Faith; and uses biblical terms and phrases that are familiar to His listeners. In these ways 'Abdu'l-Bahá enables Christian audiences to relate to the Bahá'í Faith.

Such points clearly illustrate that 'Abdu'l-Bahá considered the Bible to offer strong support for the Bahá'í Faith. Moreover, He was never embarrassed by His staunch faith in Christ and the Bible. When 'Abdu'l-Bahá was invited to speak at a synagogue in Washington, D.C., He even urged His Jewish audience to accept Christ (*Promulgation* 402–10)!

Studying 'Abdu'l-Bahá's approach will help us develop the ability to reason from the Bible in order to demonstrate the truth of Bahá'u'lláh's claims. Such an approach should prove very effective in discussions with any Christian who believes that the Bible is the inspired Word of God and who is willing to turn to the Bible when trying to make important decisions of faith. In addition to studying the talks of 'Abdu'l-Bahá, we should study the *Kitáb-i-Íqán*,[2] which also provides a clear model of reasoning from Scripture.

A METHOD FOUND IN THE *KITÁB-I-ÍQÁN*

Shoghi Effendi tells us that if we study the *Kitáb-i-Íqán* it will "infinitely enhance the teaching work in the West."[3] No doubt one reason why he makes this assertion is that this Book shows us how to present evidence. In the *Kitáb-i-Íqán* Bahá'u'lláh is

2. The *Kitáb-i-Íqán* (Arabic for "The Book of Certitude") is a book Bahá'u'lláh wrote in 1862 in the "space of two days and two nights" and "in fulfillment of the prophecy of the Báb, who had specifically stated that the Promised One would complete the text of the unfinished Persian Bayán, and in reply to the questions addressed to Bahá'u'lláh by the as yet unconverted maternal uncle of the Báb" (Shoghi Effendi, *God Passes By* 138).

3. "The Guardian Translates the Tablet of 'Iqan", in *Bahá'í News*, 46 (Nov. 1930) 2, a letter written on behalf of Shoghi Effendi to the National Spiritual Assembly of the Bahá'ís of the United States.

speaking primarily to a Muslim audience, so He uses their holy Book, the Qur'án, to advance a number of arguments supporting the claims of the Báb, the Founder of the Bábí religion and Herald of the Bahá'í Faith. His presentation can be briefly summarized in three essential steps. Bahá'u'lláh:

- demonstrates His acceptance that the Qur'án is the Word of God and an unerring source of guidance (*Kitáb-i-Íqán* 201–2);
- demonstrates which criteria are acceptable and in accordance with Scripture (*Kitáb-i-Íqán* 204–15, 227, 233); and
- demonstrates the validity of the Báb's claims by applying the scriptural criteria of the Qur'án, the same criteria Muḥammad used to demonstrate the truth of His own mission (*Kitáb-i-Íqán* 204–21).

The following chapters of *Preparing for a Bahá'í/Christian Dialogue* will closely follow the same approach, that is, we will learn to: (1) demonstrate our acceptance of the Bible as the Word of God,[4] (2) show which criteria are biblically acceptable, and (3) use the criteria of the Bible to establish Bahá'u'lláh as the latest Manifestation of God.

THE LIMITATIONS OF THE METHOD OF *PREPARING FOR A BAHÁ'Í/CHRISTIAN DIALOGUE*

A few words should be said about the limitations of the method of argument described in the *Preparing for a Bahá'í/ Christian Dialogue* series. Many readers will wonder whether reasoning from Scripture is appropriate in every discussion with every Christian. The answer is no. The general approach presented in this book is intended for Bahá'ís primarily

4. The Bahá'í acceptance of the Bible will be discussed in Chapter 3.

addressing conservative Christians who interpret the Bible literally and regard it to be the Word of God.

There are many different types of Christians, such as Catholics, the many Protestant denominations, those who are very conservative and those who are very liberal, and so on. No single approach can succeed with everyone. Some Christians rely on their Bibles more than others; some turn to their priests or ministers for guidance; still others take a more philosophical approach to religion. However, it is very important to avoid stereotyping Christians by denomination. People's beliefs are often influenced by a variety of factors. For example, some Christians' beliefs about Christ may reflect those of the congregation to which they belong, while their beliefs about prophecy may be influenced by an extremely conservative evangelical television ministry or a book recommended by a friend.

For these reasons it is best to address each Christian according to his or her particular outlook and interests. We can do this most effectively by beginning with a general conversation (when possible) in which we ask what the person's view of the Bible is and whether he or she would feel comfortable discussing it with us. If the person wishes to talk, we are in an excellent position to begin establishing the areas of common ground that are essential to opening a Bahá'í/Christian dialogue, and our advance preparations may be of great help.

3

MUTUAL ACCEPTANCE

THE RELIABILITY OF THE BIBLE

Chapter 1 discussed the importance of knowing the Bible and relying on it in our dialogues with Christians, but we may wonder whether the Bible is really a reliable Book. Some scholars question the divine inspiration of many portions of the Bible and suggest that certain verses have been added and others deleted. Others contend that the Apostles misunderstood Christ and spread teachings that were at variance with what He originally intended.[5] If these views are true, we may wonder why a Bahá'í should study the Bible. One response is

5. There is a great deal of popular misunderstanding about the field of research known as higher biblical criticism (or literary biblical criticism) and its findings. Scholars who question traditional views, beginning their investigations with different assumptions and using different principles to discover the meaning of the Scriptures, are not necessarily antagonistic to the Bible. The subject is complex and has a turbulent history. Many of the controversial works on the subject, especially those written during the nineteenth century, centered on various theories, some of which were erroneous while others rightly overturned certain orthodox beliefs. Traditional Christians generally held that the Bible was a literal account of human history. When modern scholars began to discredit this view, people began to assume that the Bible was simply unreliable. More recently, some scholars have argued that the Bible should be appreciated for its symbolism and its use of stories to present spiritual truths. Readers who wish to acquaint themselves with some of the writings of such scholars might begin with the following books: *Contemporary*

that the adoption of such views by Bahá'ís would be contrary to the writings of Bahá'u'lláh. Moreover, if we based our presentation of the Bahá'í Faith on such a viewpoint, we would be unlikely to convince those Christians who consider the Bible to be the reliable Word of God. Although we will not enter the controversy over the Bible's accuracy and authenticity here, we will discuss what the Bahá'í writings actually say about the Bible.

THE BIBLE AS THE WORD OF GOD

When we consider whether the Bible is the Word of God, we find that, in an attempt to understand apparent differences between Christian doctrines and Bahá'í teachings, Bahá'ís generally take two divergent views toward the Bible and Christianity. One view seeks to explain the differences by asserting that the Bible is unreliable and full of errors, omissions, and additions, and cannot be considered the Word of God. Bahá'ís who accept this view assert that, because the Bible is unreliable, Christians have naturally formed incorrect doctrines. Such Bahá'ís selectively cite modern scholarly biblical criticism that supports this view.[6]

Thinking about Jesus, an anthology compiled by Thomas S. Kepler. Kepler presents a variety of opinions about the nature of Jesus and His mission, from works by authors who employ modern biblical criticism and who address both historical and theological questions. Kepler includes works by such influential writers as Rudolf Bultman, Reinhold Niebuhr, Albert Schweitzer and Paul Tillich. *Critical Quest of Jesus* by Charles C. Anderson and *Finding the Historical Jesus* by James Peter examine and present some of the weaknesses of modern critical research into the life of Jesus.

6. It is unfortunate that some Bahá'í scholars, most notably Udo Schaefer (see *The Light Shineth in Darkness* 1–109), have chosen in particular to write unfavorably about Paul. See also "The Quest for the Metaphysical Jesus" by William S. Hatcher in *World Order* (12. 4 [Summer 1978]: 35–42 and "The Deification of Jesus" by Jack McLean, also in *World Order* (14. 3 and 4 [Spring/ Summer 1980]: 23–45. These articles sparked some controversy in subsequent letters to the editors. At that time, Schaefer, Hatcher and McLean

The second view asserts that the Bible is the Word of God and is, therefore, a reliable source of spiritual guidance. Bahá'ís who accept this idea suggest that some Christians have misunderstood and misinterpreted the Bible. This misunderstanding, in turn, has resulted in the apparent differences between Christian doctrines and the Bahá'í teachings. Such Bahá'ís believe the few errors in the Bible have not significantly altered its spiritual message. As evidence, they point to passages in the Bahá'í writings which seem to indicate plainly that the Bible is the Word of God and that it has been misinterpreted. They substantiate their view by reinterpreting the Bible in the light of Bahá'u'lláh's Revelation to demonstrate the harmony between the Bible and the Bahá'í Scriptures. *Preparing for a Bahá'í/Christian Dialogue* takes the latter point of view, that is, the Bible is, indeed, the Word of God.[7]

In the *Kitáb-i-Íqán*, Bahá'u'lláh writes about the importance of attaining to what He calls the "City of God" or the "City of Certitude" (196–8). He writes:

> That city is none other than the Word of God revealed in every age and dispensation. In the days of Moses it was the Pentateuch; in the days of Jesus the Gospel. (*Kitáb-i-Íqán* 199)

appear to have assumed largely that Christian interpretations of Paul's letters are true to Paul's intentions. Rather than reexamining Paul's writings in the light of the Bahá'í Revelation, these authors for the most part repeat the views of Paul's critics. The best observations published on this subject in *World Order* were expressed by Juan Ricardo Cole, in "Interchange: Letters from and to the Editor" (13. 2 [Winter 1978–79]: 7–8).

7. Shoghi Effendi states that "the Qur'án, the Bible, and our own Scriptures" can be "considered authentic Books" (*Lights of Guidance* 380). This writer is well aware of how many scholars – both Bahá'í and non-Bahá'í – will be dismayed by the position this book takes with regard to the inspiration of the Bible. Much of this stems from how the terminology is understood and defined. The distinction between the authentication of the Bible and the Bible's actual authenticity, along with conservative Christian beliefs about the Bible, will be examined more thoroughly in the next volume of *Preparing for a Bahá'í/Christian Dialogue* entitled *Understanding Christian Beliefs*.

This passage clearly indicates that the Pentateuch (the message found in the first five books of the Old Testament) and the Gospel (the message found in the New Testament) are the Word of God. Those who question the divine inspiration of the Bible may argue that it is more accurate to say the Gospel *contains* the Word of God rather than *is* the Word of God. However, the Guardian has rendered the original Persian of Bahá'u'lláh to state that "that city [the Gospel] is ... the Word of God," and therefore it must be accepted as a legitimate expression of the Bahá'í point of view. If we wish to accurately represent the Bahá'í teachings, we should not seek to extend the applicability of such terms beyond the standard found in the authoritative Bahá'í writings. Understanding and accepting these points is essential to our undertaking of successful Bahá'í/Christian dialogues.

Bahá'u'lláh's defense of the Bible

In the *Kitáb-i-Íqán* Bahá'u'lláh presents a defense of the Bible, in response to Muslim arguments against its authenticity.[8] He specifically addresses the assertion by some Muslims that certain words in the Bible have been intentionally effaced:

> Some maintain that Jewish and Christian divines have effaced from the Book such verses as extol and magnify the countenance of Muḥammad, and instead thereof have inserted the contrary. How utterly vain and false are these words! Can a man who believeth in a book, and deemeth it to be inspired by God, mutilate it? (*Kitáb-i-Íqán* 86)

8. Concerning Muslim scholars who hold to a radical criticism of the New Testament, see *Jesus in the Qur'án* by Geoffrey Parrinder, 146–7. Also, *The Encyclopedia of Islam*, new edition, edited by B. Lewis, Menage, Pellat and Schacht, 3:1207, and *The Spirit of Eastern Christendom 600–1700* by Jaroslav Pelikan, 2:236–7.

Muslims who failed to understand the truth of the Bible and how it should be interpreted argued that Muḥammad Himself stated that the Bible had been corrupted. However, Bahá'u'lláh explains that the corruption of the text that has occurred pertains not to the effacing of the words but to "the interpretation of God's holy Book in accordance with their [the Muslim divines'] idle imaginings and vain desires" (*Kitáb-i-Íqán* 86).

With specific reference to the Gospel, Bahá'u'lláh points out that Muḥammad could not have meant that the Scripture was corrupted, as some Muslims have assumed, because the Qur'án affirms its truth:

> Every discerning observer will recognize that in the Dispensation of the Qur'án both the Book and the Cause of Jesus were confirmed. (*Kitáb-i-Íqán* 20)

Referring specifically to the Gospel, Bahá'u'lláh again writes:

> We have also heard a number of the foolish of the earth assert that the genuine text of the heavenly Gospel doth not exist amongst the Christians ... How grievously they have erred! How oblivious of the fact that such a statement imputeth the gravest injustice and tyranny to a gracious and loving Providence! (*Kitáb-i-Íqán* 89)

If we ponder the implications of the words, "a gracious and loving Providence," we find little cause to question how the Gospel has managed to survive over the centuries. Bahá'u'lláh tells us that it would be inconsistent with the grace and mercy of God to cause "His holy Book, His most great testimony amongst His creatures, to disappear" (*Kitáb-i-Íqán* 89).

Thus, we find in the *Kitáb-i-Íqán* a forceful defense of the Bible by Bahá'u'lláh Himself.

'Abdu'l-Bahá's view of the Bible

'Abdu'l-Bahá also defends the Bible. When 'Abdu'l-Bahá was in England, the Reverend R. J. Campbell, minister of London's City Temple, invited 'Abdu'l-Bahá to speak to his congregation. 'Abdu'l-Bahá took this opportunity to demonstrate His attitude toward the Bible. Upon invitation, He inscribed the pulpit Bible with the words:

> This book is the Holy Book of God, of celestial Inspiration. It is the Bible of Salvation, the Noble Gospel. It is the mystery of the Kingdom and its light. It is the Divine Bounty, the sign of the guidance of God – 'Abdu'l-Bahá 'Abbás. (Balyuzi, *'Abdu'l-Bahá* 17)

'Abdu'l-Bahá's interpretation of the Qur'ánic view of the Bible

In addition to the passages already examined from the writings of Bahá'u'lláh and 'Abdu'l-Bahá, there are two particularly significant passages in the talks of 'Abdu'l-Bahá concerning the Prophet Muḥammad's view of the Bible. In both examples 'Abdu'l-Bahá asserts Muḥammad's support and confirmation of the Old and New Testaments as the Word of God, a fact not well known among Christians. 'Abdu'l-Bahá says:

> it is significant and convincing that when Muḥammad proclaimed His work and mission, His first objection to His own followers was, "Why have you not believed on Jesus Christ? Why have you not accepted the Gospel? Why have you not believed in Moses? Why have you not followed the precepts of the Old Testament? Why have you not understood the prophets of Israel? Why have you not believed in the disciples of Christ? The first duty incumbent upon ye, O Arabians, is to accept and believe

in these. You must consider Moses as a Prophet. You must accept Jesus Christ as the Word of God. You must know the Old and the New Testaments as the Word of God. (*Promulgation* 201)

In another talk, 'Abdu'l-Bahá cites Muḥammad's statement that "the Bible is the Book of God":

In the Qur'án we read that Muḥammad spoke to his followers, saying: "Why do you not believe in Christ, and in the Gospel? Why will you not accept Moses and the Prophets, for surely the Bible is the Book of God?" (*Paris Talks* 47)

This passage is particularly significant because it is so all-inclusive. It is well worth examining carefully. Paraphrasing passages from the Qur'án, "Why have you not believed in the disciples of Christ?," strongly suggests that 'Abdu'l-Bahá affirms the importance Muḥammad placed on the disciples' writings. He also quotes Muḥammad as stating that both the Old and New Testaments are "the Word of God," while in the second passage He not only mentions Moses but also states "and the Prophets." Thus 'Abdu'l-Bahá emphasizes the breadth of Muḥammad's affirmation that "the Bible is the Book of God."

THE MEANING OF THE WORD 'GOSPEL'

Before discussing how we can use the Bible in Bahá'í/Christian dialogues, we must clear up questions about the meaning of the word *Gospel*. When Bahá'u'lláh refers in the *Kitáb-i-Íqán* to "the genuine text of the heavenly Gospel" (89), does He mean only the words of Christ, or does He mean the first four Books of the New Testament (often referred to as the Gospels), or does He mean the entire New Testament, which would include the other writings of the Apostles? An examination of the term 'Gospel' in the Bahá'í writings, the Qur'án, and the Bible suggests that the term refers to the entire New Testament.

In the original Greek, the word 'Gospel' means 'good news' or 'glad tidings.' The word simply refers to the message of Christ or to the text containing that message. Furthermore, there is no use of the plural form 'Gospels' in the New Testament. Jesus used the term 'Gospel' at a time when no written Gospel existed (Mark 1:14–15). The Apostle Paul suggests that 'Gospel' means the message originating with Christ that reveals the righteousness of God and leads to salvation (Rom. 1:16–17). Paul says of himself, "I have fully preached the gospel of Christ" (Rom. 15:19). Nowhere in the New Testament is there any use of the term 'Gospel' that would suggest that its meaning should be restricted to only the words attributed to Christ or any other exclusive portion of the New Testament. In reality the Gospel of Christ is one Gospel. The first four Books of the New Testament (Matthew, Mark, Luke, and John) are essentially variations on the same theme, the mission of Jesus.[9]

In the Bahá'í writings there are some instances where Bahá'u'lláh uses the plural form 'Gospels' to refer to the first four Books of the New Testament (e.g. *Kitáb-i-Íqán* 22, 25). In these instances He is directing the reader to specific themes mentioned in those Books. Most other references in the writings of Bahá'u'lláh, 'Abdu'l-Bahá, and Shoghi Effendi, like those in the Bible and the Qur'án, seem to use 'Gospel' in a way that does not suggest a meaning limited to just the first four Books of the New Testament.

It is also important to clear up any questions we may have about the other writings of the Apostles included in the New Testament. Whatever the distinction between the words attributed to Christ and the other writings of His Apostles, the

9. For this reason some Christian scholars use the term "fourfold Gospel" to refer collectively to those Books.

position of the Apostles and their writings is exalted. 'Abdu'l-Bahá wrote:

> It is evident that the Letter is a member of the Word, and this membership in the Word signifieth that the Letter is dependent for its value on the Word, that is, it deriveth its grace from the Word; it has a spiritual kinship with the Word, and is accounted an integral part of the Word. The Apostles were even as Letters, and Christ was the essence of the Word Itself; and the meaning of the Word, which is grace everlasting, cast a splendor on those Letters. Again, since the Letter is a member of the Word, it therefore, in its inner meaning, is consonant with the Word. (*Selections from the Writings of 'Abdu'l-Bahá* 60)

To be "consonant" is to be in agreement, accordance or harmony. 'Abdu'l-Bahá's comment establishes that, from a Bahá'í point of view, the Apostles' are in harmony with Christ and, hence, their writings should be respected. Understanding such harmony is particularly important with regard to the Apostle Paul. Since Paul's writings comprise a large portion of the New Testament, it is essential that Bahá'ís avoid unfairly criticizing or trying to discredit him, as some scholars have. Such criticism undermines much of the evidence available to substantiate Bahá'í beliefs, and creates an unnecessary impediment between Bahá'ís and the vast majority of Christians who believe that Paul is an Apostle of Christ. 'Abdu'l-Bahá characterized Saint Paul as one who "became heavenly" and as "a divine philosopher" (Balyuzi, *'Abdu'l-Bahá* 354) who "was in close embrace with" Christ (*Tablets of 'Abdu'l-Bahá Abbas* 720), and "became His most faithful servant" (*Paris Talks* 147).

All of the points we have thus far discussed – the authority of the Bible, the meaning of the word 'Gospel,' the writings of the Apostles – are complex issues. The purpose here is simply to present some of the basic and representative statements

found in the authoritative Bahá'í writings and talks of 'Abdu'l-
Bahá so that we can perceive the spirit in which the Bahá'í
Faith regards the Bible. In later chapters, and especially in
Volume Two, these issues will be examined in greater depth.
The present information, however, provides us with the neces-
sary background to proceed through the rest of Volume One.

USING THE BIBLE IN BAHÁ'Í/CHRISTIAN DIALOGUES

The more closely we study what the Bahá'í writings say about
the Bible, the more we will realize that the importance of
accepting the Bible and appreciating its sacredness cannot be
overstated. This realization will inspire in us appropriate reverence for the Christian Scriptures which, in turn, will also
help us convey our sincerity to Christians. The depth of such
convictions is important when we seek to establish areas of
agreement in our dialogues with Christians.

Accepting the Bible as the Word of God will provide a mutually agreed upon source of criteria for discussing with Christians the truth of the Bahá'í Faith. If Bahá'ís fail to recognize
the Bible as the Word of God, we cannot accurately represent
the teachings of the Bahá'í Faith, and we will have given up a
large foundation of scriptural evidence with which the Bahá'í
Faith can be substantiated.

Since the Bible is the Word of God, we should not hesitate
to refer to it if a Christian wishes to do so. In fact, we should
encourage Christians to judge the Bahá'í Faith according to
the standard set in the Bible.[10]

10. It is worth noting that the Qur'án states that "they who have received
the Gospel" should "judge according to what God hath revealed therein: and
who so judgeth not according to what God hath revealed they are transgres-
sors" (*The Koran*, trans. George Sale, 105; cf. *Qur'án* 5:47, Yusuf Ali's trans.).
Similarly, Bahá'u'lláh writes, "In mine hand I carry the testimony of God, your
Lord and the Lord of your sires of old. Weigh it with the just Balance that ye
possess, the Balance of the testimony of the Prophets and Messengers of God.
If ye find it to be established in truth, if ye believe it to be of God, beware, then,

The historian Nabíl records in his narrative, *The Dawn-Breakers*, an example of Bahá'u'lláh's confidence in Scripture. Nabíl writes that after Bahá'u'lláh presented His message to Mullá Muḥammad, the following occurred:

> Mullá Muḥammad disparagingly remarked: "I undertake no action unless I first consult the Qur'án. I have invariably, on such occasions, followed the practice of invoking the aid of God and His blessings; of opening at random His sacred Book, and of consulting the first verse of the particular page upon which my eyes chance to fall. From the nature of that verse I can judge the wisdom and the advisability of my contemplated course of action." Finding that Bahá'u'lláh was not inclined to refuse him his request, the mujtahid [Mullá Muḥammad] called for a copy of the Qur'án, opened and closed it again, refusing to reveal the nature of the verse to those who were present. All he said was this: "I have consulted the Book of God, and deem it inadvisable to proceed further with this matter." A few agreed with him; the rest, for the most part, did not fail to recognize the fear which those words implied. Bahá'u'lláh, disinclined to cause him further embarrassment, arose and, asking to be excused, bade him a cordial farewell. (*Dawn-Breakers* 117)

Bahá'u'lláh's response in this example exemplifies the attitude we should have toward Christians. Since Bahá'u'lláh intended to share with Mullá Muḥammad the Báb's word, which was the Word of God, Bahá'u'lláh had nothing to fear from the Qur'án. Both the Báb's word and the Qur'án are the Word of God; hence, neither can rightly be an obstruction to the truth of the other. Similarly, since the Bible is the Word of God, Bahá'ís should not fear Christians who refer to it; rather it

least ye cavil at it, and render your works vain". (Bahá'u'lláh, *Gleanings* 281). See also, Hohn 5:46–7.

should be welcomed as a source of confirmation of the truth of
Bahá'u'lláh. Bahá'u'lláh Himself asked Christians:

> Read ye the Evangel [the Gospel of Jesus] and yet refuse
> to acknowledge the All-Glorious Lord? This indeed be-
> seemeth you not, O concourse of learned men! (Shoghi
> Effendi, *Promised Day* 103)

Of course, when we refer to the Scriptures for guidance, it is
advisable to use a sounder method than that practiced by
Mullá Muḥammad.[11]

Keep in mind that mutual acceptance requires more than
simply accepting the Bible as a divinely inspired Book. We
must try to grasp the essence of the Bible's ultimate purpose
and meaning if we are to establish mutual agreement with the
Christians we encounter. The Bible teaches, among many
other eternal spiritual truths, that our purpose is to love God,
to love one another, to help others, and to be humble. We
should approach Christians with the understanding that we all
share a common belief in these spiritual truths. Conflict,
criticism, or attempts to exalt ourselves over others can ob-
scure our similarities. Consequently, we must try to avoid
contentious arguments and aim to build mutual understanding upon those shared values and beliefs. In the next chapter
we will show how our acceptance of the Bible provides us with
a shared source of very specific evidence supporting the claims
of Bahá'u'lláh.

11. This method of guidance is known as 'istikhárih' in Islam and is
discouraged in the Bahá'í Faith. See *Consultation* 17.

4

COMMON CRITERIA

Mutual acceptance of the Bible as the Word of God provides a positive basis on which we can begin a Bahá'í/Christian dialogue. Yet where do we begin? It is clear that the Bible is our ally, but we need to know how to refer to it wisely and appropriately in our discussions. This chapter, drawing on the model from the *Kitáb-i-Íqán* outlined in Chapter 2, examines some specific biblical criteria that support the truth of Bahá'u'lláh's claims. However, first we need to examine why the Word of God should be the basis of our beliefs and what differentiates human from divine standards for ascertaining the truth.

THE BASIS OF OUR BELIEFS

People recognize religious truth for a variety of reasons. However, if they base their beliefs solely on human standardf of judgment, the passage of time may prove the basis for their judgment faulty and eventually erode their beliefs, even though such standards may have no bearing on truth. Hence the great lesson of Saint Paul's words, "the wisdom of this world is foolishness with God" (1 Cor. 3:19). By human standards is simply meant those things that do not pertain to the recognition of divine attributes and which do not accord with the standards revealed in Scripture.

It is important to be aware of how we can recognize truth. All things in creation have their own particular attributes by which they are recognized and known; these attributes determine the criteria we use to identify and understand them. For example, we know the sun by its light and heat. We cannot, however, use the same set of criteria for recognizing the ocean. Likewise, a Manifestation of God is known by particular qualities and cannot be judged by standards that have no relation to these specific qualities.

Foremost among the attributes of a Manifestation of God is His Word, for it is this Word that renews and spiritualizes the hearts of humankind, God's essential purpose in sending Messengers. In the Bible it is recorded:

Man shall not live by bread alone, but by every word of God. (Luke 4:4, cf. Deut. 8:3)

This passage points out that our spiritual life depends on the Word of God. In many passages Bahá'u'lláh also emphasizes humanity's enduring need for the Word of God. In fact, this need is the very reason that God, out of His grace, has continuously sent Manifestations in every age. Hence, He writes that the Word "hath never been withheld from the world of being" (*Tablets of Bahá'u'lláh* 140–1).[12]

Therefore, the Word of God is the standard by which we recognize God's Messengers and is the means by which truth is known after the Messengers have ascended. It is to Scripture that we should turn for spiritual guidance. Bahá'u'lláh assures us that Scriptures, left behind by a Messenger of God to guide humankind until the next Manifestation appears, are the testimony of the Messenger:

How could God, when once the Day-star of the beauty of Jesus had disappeared from the sight of His people, and

12. See, for example, *Kitáb-i-Íqán*, 14, 136–7.

ascended unto the fourth heaven,[13] cause His holy Book, His most great testimony amongst His creatures, to disappear also? What would be left to that people to cling to from the setting of the day-star of Jesus until the rise of the sun of the Muḥammadan Dispensation? (*Kitáb-i-Íqán 89*)

The Word of God, then, given by the Messenger in His Book, forms the surest standard for recognizing truth, the surest basis for belief. This is because it reveals the divine qualities which inform us that it is from God.

HUMAN VERSUS DIVINE STANDARDS

It will help our study of the Word of God if we examine the difference between human and divine standards. God sets the standard by sending Messengers and by revealing holy Books. The purpose of these Messengers and divine Books is to reveal the attributes of God, to transform our lives, to give us spiritual guidance. The truth of the Prophets must, therefore, be judged by the existence of these divine qualities. Bahá'u'lláh proclaims the Book of God as the divine standard with these words:

13. The 'fourth heaven' is a term used by followers of the Shí'ah sect of Islam. In Islamic belief, it is commonly held that there are seven heavens (see Qur'án 23:17), and according to popular belief, Jesus is said to reside in the fourth heaven. Bahá'u'lláh appears to be using this term in order to make His point in the context of the beliefs of the Muslims to whom He is speaking. The meaning of the fourth heaven is difficult to ascertain. Shí'ah beliefs about the nature and characteristics of the heavens are not consistent, nor are all such beliefs clearly based on the Qur'án. The concept is based more on traditions and popular beliefs which have similarities to ideas that appear to go back at least as far as Ptolemy. (See *Dictionary of Islam* by Thomas Patrick Hughes 170.) The Old Testament suggests several heavens (Deut. 10:14), but Rabinnical literature speaks of seven and even ten heavens. (See *The Jewish Encyclopedia*, Isidore Singer, 6: 298, and 1: 591–92.) Paul once mentions the third heaven (2 Cor. 12:2), but he does not provide any explanation.

O leaders of religion! Weigh not the Book of God with such standards and sciences as are current amongst you, for the Book itself is the unerring balance established amongst men. In this most perfect balance whatsoever the peoples and kindreds of the earth possess must be weighed, while the measure of its weight should be tested according to its own standard, did ye but know it. (*Synopsis* 22)

In particular, we should not judge Scripture merely by what others think about it, by its grammatical style, or by whether or not it explains certain material principles. Nor should we discount it on historical or cultural grounds, or on the grounds that our interpretation of it agrees with this scientific theory or another. Our goal should be to ascertain its spiritual value.

The early history of the Bahá'í Faith provides an example of an individual's use of non-scriptural criteria to judge a Prophet. The first person to believe in the Báb[14] was Mullá Husayn.[15] Because he believed that the time for the appearance of God's promised Messenger was at hand, he set out on a personal quest to find the Promised One. In his mind he had established two criteria by which he intended to judge the truth of anyone who might claim to be the Promised One. Neither criterion was based on Scripture. Mullá Husayn's account is related by Mírzá Ahmad-i-Qazvíní and recorded by Nabíl in *The Dawn-Breakers:*

The first [criterion] was a treatise which I had myself

14. The Báb, the Prophet-Herald of the Bahá'í Faith, is believed to be the return in Spirit of the Prophet Elijah, of John the Baptist, and of the Twelfth Imam awaited by Muslims. Shoghi Effendi writes that the Báb is the "independent Author of a divinely revealed Dispensation" and the "Herald of a new Era and the Inaugurator of a great universal prophetic cycle" (*God Passes By* 57).

15. Mullá Husayn was an Islamic priest who was the first to believe in the Báb. He was appointed a disciple, or "Letter of the Living", by the Báb and suffered martyrdom on 2 February 1849, at the age of thirty-five.

composed, bearing upon the abstruse and hidden teachings propounded by <u>Sh</u>ay<u>kh</u> Aḥmad and Siyyid Káẓim[16]. Whoever seemed to me capable of unraveling the mysterious allusions made in that treatise, to him I would next submit my second request, and would ask him to reveal, without the least hesitation or reflection, a commentary on the Súrih of Joseph,[17] in a style and language entirely different from the prevailing standards of the time. (*Dawn-Breakers* 59)

Even though the Báb readily complied with Mullá Ḥusayn's two tests, He strongly admonished him afterward:

The all-encompassing grace of God has saved you. It is for God to test His servants, and not for His servants to judge Him in accordance with their deficient standards. (*Dawn-Breakers* 61)

It appears that Mullá Ḥusayn was absorbed in issues of academic learning. What if the Báb had not chosen to answer these types of questions? Mullá Ḥusayn was risking his faith by resting it on things that may never have come to pass and which were in no way required of the Báb. Nabíl's account clearly emphasizes the importance of relying on the divine standard, the recognition of the spiritual perfections revealed in the Manifestation's life and teachings.

---

16. <u>Sh</u>ay<u>kh</u> Aḥmad-i-Aḥsá'í (1753–1834) and his successor, Siyyid Kazim-i-Ra<u>sh</u>t (1793–1843), were prominent Muslims (perhaps comparable in some respects to nineteenth century Christians adventists) believed by Bahá'ís to have heralded the Báb and Bahá'u'lláh. See *Dawn-Breakers* 1–46.

17. "The Súrih (or chapter) of Joseph" refers to the twelfth chapter of the Qur'án. The Báb's commentary on this chapter is entitled *Qayyúmu'l-Asmá'*. See Shoghi Effendi, *God Passes By* 23. Because of statements made by his teacher, Siyyid Kázim, Mullá Ḥusayn chose the interpretation of the Súrih of Joseph as one of the criteria by which he would know the Promised One. See *Dawn-Breakers* 59.

SPECIFIC CRITERIA FROM THE BIBLE

Now we are ready to turn to several passages in the New Testament that illustrate how effective the Word of God can be in helping us identify and establish truth. More specifically, the verses selected can be used to help us establish that Bahá'u'lláh is of God.

The author of the first epistle of John distinguishes between what is "the Spirit of God" and what "is not of God" (1 John 4:2,3). He begins with a counsel to search out the truth before believing:

> Beloved, do not believe every spirit, but test the spirits, whether they are of God; because many false prophets have gone out into the world. (1 John 4:1)

The following two verses suggest a test by which the distinction between who is and who is not of God can be made. The text also defines the Antichrist:

> By this you know the Spirit of God: Every spirit that confesses that Jesus Christ has come in the flesh is of God, and every spirit that does not confess that Jesus Christ has come in the flesh is not of God. And this is the *spirit* of the Antichrist,[18] which you have heard was coming, and is now already in the world. (1 John 4:2-3)[19]

18. The term "Antichrist" or "Antichrists" appears only five times in the Bible, (twice in) 1 John 2:18; 1 John 2:22; 1 John 4:3; and 2 John 7. It is interesting to note that the term generally refers to one person but in one instance refers to "many antichrists" (1 John 2:18). Some Christians believe the Antichrist is synonymous with the "man of sin" (2 Thess. 2:3) and the "beast" (Rev. 13), and some believe these verses signify an individual who will arise to be Christ's main adversary when He returns. Others believe the Antichrist will lead armies of evildoers and deceived people against the forces of Christ in an epic battle that will precede the establishment of the Kingdom of God on earth. Such views have been used to interpret current political events and have been popularized by writers such as Hal Lindsey and Mike Evans. The Bahá'í point of view is expressed in a letter to an individual Bahá'í on behalf of Shoghi Effendi: "We do not believe in Anti-Christ in the sense the Christians do.

In this verse the recognition of Jesus' divinity is set forth as a test in itself. To say that Jesus came in the flesh is to say that Jesus of Nazareth was not just a great man; He was the Son of God, the Christ – an historical figure who walked and taught on the earth.

There can be no mistake that Bahá'u'lláh affirms the truth of Jesus' divinity. In numerous passages Bahá'u'lláh clearly confesses that Jesus was the Christ in the flesh. For example, Bahá'u'lláh refers to Jesus' death on the cross and how it changed the world:

> Know thou that when the Son of Man yielded up His breath to God, the whole creation wept with a great weeping. By sacrificing Himself, however, a fresh capacity was infused into all created things. Its evidences, as witnessed in all the peoples of the earth, are now manifest before thee. (*Gleanings* 85)

Furthermore, Bahá'u'lláh writes:

> Reflect how Jesus, the Spirit of God, was, notwithstanding His extreme meekness and perfect tenderheartedness, treated by His enemies. So fierce was the opposition which He, the Essence of Being and Lord of the visible and invisible, had to face, that He had nowhere to lay His head. He wandered continually from place to place, deprived of a permanent abode. (*Gleanings* 57)

Anyone who violently and determinedly sought to oppose the Manifestation could be called an 'anti-Christ,' such as the Vazír in the Báb's day, Ḥájí Mírzá Aqásí (*Lights of Guidance* 367–8).

19. Some Christian writers do not believe that the verse "Jesus Christ has come in the flesh" (1 John 4:2) indicates simply that Jesus is the Christ or Messiah in the flesh. The difficulty arises over what is the Messiah and what "in the flesh" means. Christian writers J.R.W. Stott and Matthew Henry involve the doctrine of incarnation, some even see 1 John 4:2 as a statement of Christian creed encompassing the resurrection of Christ. Thus a simple criterion becomes a complex test of doctrinal purity. See, for example, J.R.W. Stott's *The Epistles of John: An Introduction and Commentary 154*.

With these declarations Bahá'u'lláh unmistakably establishes, by a New Testament criterion (confessing that Jesus came in the flesh), that He is "of God" and is not the Antichrist.

When we turn to the writings of Paul, we find a similar criterion, this one establishing that Bahá'u'lláh speaks by the Holy Spirit. Paul writes:

> Therefore I make known to you that no one speaking by the Spirit of God calls Jesus accursed, and no one can say that Jesus is Lord except by the Holy Spirit. (1 Cor. 12:3)

Bahá'u'lláh speaks of Jesus Christ not only as the "Lord of the visible and invisible" (*Gleanings* 57) but also as "the Lord of all being" (*Epistle* 100). This is biblical proof, not merely a human assertion, that Bahá'u'lláh speaks by the Holy Spirit.

Another significant scriptural criterion that can be used to establish whether Bahá'u'lláh is of God is found in the Gospel of Matthew, where Christ is quoted as saying:

> Beware of false prophets, who come to you in sheep's clothing, but inwardly they are ravenous wolves. You will know them by their fruits. Do men gather grapes from thornbushes or figs from thistles? Even so, every good tree bears good fruit, but a bad tree bears bad fruit. A good tree cannot bear bad fruit, nor *can* a bad tree bear good fruit. Every tree that does not bear good fruit is cut down and thrown into the fire. Therefore by their fruits you will know them. (Matt. 7:15–20)[20]

20. The criterion offered by Christ in chapter 7 of Matthew is applicable to false prophets – whether they are false prophets in the sense of those who minister in the church or in the sense of those who lay claim to Messianic Prophethood, because both are known by their qualities or fruits. However, one line of reasoning suggests interpreting this verse as referring to Prophethood in the Messianic sense. Christ states, "A good tree cannot bear bad fruit, nor can a bad tree bear good fruit" (Matt. 7:18). From a Bahá'í point of view, one of the essential differences between the Prophets, or Manifestations of God, and humankind is that the Prophets are "pure from every sin,

These verses are especially important because they are crucial to recognizing a true Prophet.[21] The term "fruits" refers to qualities or attributes. Paul also uses the term "fruit" to refer to the attributes of Christians who walk not in the flesh, but in the Spirit:

> But the fruit of the Spirit is love, joy, peace, long-suffering, kindness, goodness, faithfulness, gentleness, self-control. (Gal. 5:22–23)

To apply Jesus Christ's counsel that "by their fruits you will know them" (Matt. 7:20), we must determine if Bahá'u'lláh's life and teachings reflect the "fruit of the Spirit." If we find in Bahá'u'lláh "all goodness, righteousness, and truth," (Gal. 5:9) He is of God.

We have seen that Paul uses the word "fruit" in the sense of qualities or attributes. In applying the criterion given by Christ in the Gospel of Matthew, we must consider not only qualities of righteousness but also the other fruits (or qualities) that characterize a Prophet of God. Christ's approach to this matter is really very simple. He asks rhetorically: "Do men gather grapes from thorn bushes or figs from thistles?" (Matt. 7:16). Hence, the type of fruit is determined by the kind of tree on which it grows. Therefore we can ask the question: Does the reality of Bahá'u'lláh's station support His claims? Is He a Prophet or simply a righteous man? Righteousness alone does

and sanctified from faults" ('Abdul'-Bahá, *Some Answered Questions* 170). Humankind, however, is not. Some may feel, therefore, that humanity's imperfect and limited nature will, in spite of its struggles toward perfection, inevitably bear bad fruit. This suggests that only the Manifestations of God are truly good trees that do not bear bad fruit. However, in this writer's opinion, it is probably unwise to interpret Christ's statement in too strict a sense.

21. The term Prophet can have three biblical meanings: (1) Messianic Prophets like Christ and Moses; (2) Prophets who upheld the teachings promulgated by Moses, such as Isaiah, Jeremiah, Ezekiel and others; and (3) individuals who simply have a gift of prophecy. These distinctions will be examined in Part Three, Chapter 9.

not prove anyone is a Prophet of God. What enables us to know that Bahá'u'lláh is a Prophet of God is that His qualities are thoroughly consistent with all His claims, which encompass more than just righteousness. We will discuss in detail the essential qualities and characteristics of Prophets (i.e., Prophets in the Messianic sense) and the validity of Bahá'u'lláh's claims in Part Three. These criteria have been mentioned in this chapter to demonstrate some specific examples which show how effective it can be to rely on the Bible.

RELYING ON THE BIBLE

Referring to the Bible to find criteria for determining the truth is much safer than relying on one's own or someone else's personal ideas. Christians may, in some discussions, present criteria that have no biblical support and that represent only personal opinion. At other times they may present criteria that are loosely based on interpretations of some particular passage or passages in the Bible. For example, a Christian may say, "I can't believe Bahá'u'lláh is who He claims to be if He does not go by the name Jesus Christ," or "I can't believe in Bahá'u'lláh if He taught anything more than what is contained in the Bible." (These questions will be considered in greater detail in Volumes Two and Three which deal with doctrines and prophecies respectively.) In such cases we should ask questions and seek to understand the basis of the other person's point of view. What biblical verses or other sources of information were used to arrive at the conclusions? Whenever possible, refer to the actual text. If the Christian does not know where in the Bible to locate support for a view, that view will naturally lose some of its force and may, in fact, increase the Christian's receptiveness to our presentations.

Courteously asking Christians to support their arguments with Scripture shows our respect for the Bible and helps keep the discussion centered on the Word of God. If the Christian can provide the verses to support the discussion, we and the

Christian can examine them to see whether such verses are applicable. However, when we refer to the Bible it is important that we do so in an appropriate spirit and with sensitivity to our audience. We should avoid quoting verses in an over aggressive manner or needlessly reciting verse numbers in a way that appears pompous and arrogant. The objective is to show our acceptance of the Bible and to discuss issues in an atmosphere of mutual inquiry.

SUMMARY

By referring to the Bible we have established a number of important points about Bahá'u'lláh and have begun to use the method with which we will continue our discussion. We have demonstrated that Bahá'u'lláh, as far as we can determine from the biblical criteria and evidence we have discussed, is of God. He is "of God" (1 John 4:2) because He teaches and acknowledges the historical truth of Jesus Christ (*Gleanings* 47, 85-6). He speaks "by the Holy Spirit" (1 Cor. 12:3) because He teaches that Jesus is "Lord" (*Epistle* 100). And, finally, we have determined from Matthew 7:15-20 that, in order to know the reality of His claims, we must examine His life and teachings.

The examples of criteria for proving Bahá'u'lláh's station presented in this chapter are only a few of the many verses that can be used; further information on this subject can be found in Part Three: Proofs. The next chapter outlines a technique that uses special methods and materials to help you prepare for and engage in Bahá'í/Christian dialogues.

5

METHODS AND
MATERIALS

Many Christians have found a simple but helpful recording technique by which they can readily locate specific biblical verses in consecutive order.[22] It is a method that can also be very useful to Bahá'ís who wish to find and use relevant verses in their discussions with Christians. This chapter will acquaint us with that method and with some books and study aids to help us examine the Bible and Christian beliefs.

MATERIALS WE WILL NEED

To use the technique described here effectively, we will need the following materials:

* *The New King James Version of the Bible*
  All biblical references in *Preparing for a Bahá'í/Christian Dialogue* are to the New King James Version, which is essentially the same as the Authorized[23] King James

---

22. The idea of using such a recording technique first occurred to the author when he received *The Christian Life New Testament*, which contains a system of outlines and notes by Porter Barrington.

23. The word "authorized" refers to the approval this edition received from King James of England in the seventeenth century. Apart from that, this designation does not in itself mean that this edition is superior to any other edition.

Version. However, archaic vocabulary, punctuation, and grammar have been updated, pronouns referring to God have been capitalized, and quotation marks have been inserted where appropriate. These features remove the difficulties of reading the King James Version and make the New King James Version easier to understand. A red-letter edition with all the words attributed to Christ printed in red is preferable, as it highlights the sequence of the Gospel dialogues.

It should be noted that some Christians object to the New King James Version. For reasons of style or scholarship, people often prefer different translations. It is important to avoid arguing over such issues; instead, welcome the diversity of scholarship and style. There are many good translations of the Bible, such as the Revised Standard Version and the New International Version. Frequently, comparisons of different translations help to clarify ambiguities of meaning. If the Christians we encounter use editions other than the New King James Version (for example, the New American Standard Version), we may find it best to adopt that edition. There is no official version of the Bible that Bahá'ís must use.

- *Green, Blue, and Yellow Highlighting Markers*
  We will use markers for highlighting specific verses. Light-colored markers that do not bleed through paper are the best for this purpose.

MAKING TOPICAL OUTLINES OF BIBLICAL THEMES

In the previous chapter we identified some biblical verses that provide criteria by which the truth of Bahá'u'lláh's claims can be judged. Now we will begin to use a four-step method to highlight and link the relevant biblical passages on this topic for easy location and use in our discussions with Christians.

- Using a *green* marker, highlight in your Bible the verses discussed in Chapter 3 that deal with criteria for judging the truth of Bahá'u'lláh's claims: 1 John 4:1–3, 1 Cor. 12:3, Matt. 7:15–20, Gal. 5:22–3, Eph. 5:9–10.

- Next to the first verse (1 John 4:1–3) write, in an abbreviated form, the number of the second verse in the sequence (1 Cor. 12:3). Write the number of the third verse next to the second verse, and so on. Write next to the last verse the number of the first verse. This will bring us full circle, referring us to a cycle of biblical verses that deal with one theme. Such a cycle of verses can serve as a simple outline of the points one might wish to cover in discussing a single theme. By locating one verse in the outline we will be able to find them all.

- Write the topic of the color-coded outline – which, in this example, can be abbreviated to "Criteria" – at the top of the page containing the verse with which we wish to begin our discussion of the criteria by which the truth of Bahá'u'lláh's station can be judged. For example, we may want to use the page containing 1 John 4:1–3 as our starting point. In addition, list each topic in the back of your Bible and, next to it, write the verse numbers for one of the verses from the outline. Highlighting the Bible in this way will make finding the verses quick and easy.

- The final step is to select a pertinent passage from the Bahá'í writings that presents the Bahá'í position most concisely and effectively. Although it is best to memorize such passages (and whatever biblical verse from the outline is most relevant), it may be helpful to add a footnote to the Bahá'í quotation at the bottom of the appropriate page in the Bible we are using. Such a footnote should give the page number of the passage in the Bahá'í writings to which we want to refer. It may also be desirable to write out the quotation in full in the back of the Bible. However, some Christians will become apprehensive if they think that Bahá'ís are inserting Bahá'í verses in the Bible, and it is preferable, therefore, to limit ourselves to the footnote.

Each of the three highlighters will be used to color-code various themes in the Bible:

> Criteria and proofs (green)
> Prophecies (blue)
> Doctrines (yellow).

Regularly using the four-step method to outline biblical passages on various topics will eventually enable us to locate the verses we want to use, even if the Bible that happens to be available does not have our special outlines. That is where study, preparation for Bahá'í/Christian dialogue, and memorization come into play.

THE EFFECTIVENESS OF MEMORIZATION

Reverently quoting from Scripture can be an extremely potent way to augment our teaching efforts. We may frequently find ourselves in situations where no Bible is available. Memorization is the best preparation for such occasions.

We will also want to memorize certain passages from the Bahá'í writings. Bahá'u'lláh tells us that memorizing verses from the Scriptures will empower our teaching efforts and will leave "no cause for vacillation."

> The sanctified souls should ponder and meditate in their hearts regarding the methods of teaching. From the texts of the wondrous, heavenly Scriptures they should memorize phrases and passages bearing on various instances, so that in the course of their speech they may recite divine verses whenever the occasion demandeth it, inasmuch as

these holy verses are the most potent elixir, the greatest and mightiest talisman. So potent is their influence that the hearer will have no cause for vacillation. (*Tablets of Bahá'u'lláh* 200)

'Abdu'l-Bahá also emphasizes the importance of memorizing Scripture to be an effective teacher:

It is very good to memorize the logical points and proofs of the Holy Books. Those proofs and evidences which establish the fact that Bahá'u'lláh is the fulfillment of the Promises of the Holy Books. These proofs ought to be collected and memorized. As soon as someone will ask you – What are your proofs – you may cry out at the top of your voice and say: "Here they are!"[24]

AIDS TO STUDYING THE BIBLE AND CHRISTIANITY

Because the Bible is such a large and complex work, it can be difficult to study. The study tips and aids suggested here are meant to simplify and ease this task. The following books are recommended but not essential. The bibliography at the back of the book lists publishers and other information that will help readers who wish to locate them.

• *Bible Concordance*
A Bible concordance enables students of the Bible to look up quickly every occurrence of any key word in the Bible. Strong's *The Exhaustive Concordance of the Bible* is readily available. It contains a Hebrew and Chaldee dictionary and a Greek dictionary, both of which contain the original word forms and their English renderings. Different concordances are available for different translations of the

24. 'Abdu'l-Bahá, quoted in Joseph H. Hannen, "With Abdul'l-Bahá in Dublin, New Hampshire", *Star of the West* 3. 11 (27 Sept.1912): 4.

Bible; however, if a concordance for the specific edition of the Bible we are using is not available, Strong's concordance is usually sufficient. Of all the tools available this is usually the most helpful.

- *A Topical Bible*
A topical Bible organizes Scripture by topic. It differs from a concordance in that it offers references to concepts as well as words. For example, we will not find the word "Trinity" in a concordance, but we can find it in a topical Bible. "Trinity" is a Christian term but not a biblical word. A large and comprehensive topical Bible is *The Zondervan Topical Bible,* which is also available in an edited and very adequate compact edition.

- *A Bible Dictionary*
When we want to find quickly the meaning of a word, concept, name, or place that we have heard a Christian mention or that we have found in the Bible, a Bible dictionary is a very useful reference tool. Many Bible dictionaries are available, such as *Unger's Bible Dictionary* by Merrill Unger, or the *New Bible Dictionary* by the Tyndale Fellowship for Biblical Research.

- *A Bible Handbook*
Many helpful Bible study books are available, but *Halley's Bible Handbook* is still one of the most widely recommended and used among conservative Christians in America. This relatively small book does not give a complete commentary, but it does give useful general information on each of the books of the Bible as well as tying in various conservative Christian beliefs and arguments.

- *Books on Christian Doctrines*
Any Bahá'í who wants to teach Christians effectively should understand Christian beliefs and doctrines.

Reading books about doctrines acquaints us with the essentials of conservative Protestant belief regarding such issues as Christ's deity, the Trinity, the doctrine of sin, the Second Coming of Christ, and so on.

Most of the Christian authors cited in *Preparing for a Bahá'í/Christian Dialogue* reflect the beliefs of conservative or moderate Protestantism.[25] Floyd H. Barackman's *Practical Christian Theology*, which is referred to in this book most frequently for doctrinal information, is respected by many prominent conservative Protestants such as Dr J. F. Walvoord, President of Dallas Theological Seminary, and Dr H. L. Willmington, Vice-President of Liberty Baptist College. Barackman teaches systematic theology at the Practical Bible Training School in New York. His book is useful for its many biblical references that support the conservative point of view and for its readability. R. A. Torrey's *What the Bible Teaches* and Dr William Evans' *Great Doctrines of the Bible* also express a moderate to conservative point of view. If you are speaking primarily with Catholics or more liberal Protestants, however, you may need to read doctrinal books expressing their points of view.[26] Doctrines are sometimes very complex and literature on the subject can be tedious. It is therefore, beneficial to start out with books or pamphlets that provide brief and simple explanations.

25. For readers unfamiliar with the distinction between liberal and conservative Christianity, William E. Hordern's *A Layman's Guide to Protestant Theology* is recommended.

26. If you encounter Christians who are disinclined toward mainstream Protestant thinking, or if you live in a predominantly Catholic area, you may wish to seek out different books on doctrines. Ask a local minister, priest, or Christian acquaintance to recommend a book that will help you to understand their doctrinal point of view. Some Bahá'ís may find of interest *The Common Catechism*, a collaborative product of both Catholic and Protestant theologians. For the studious reader, this ecumenical book is useful in that it examines areas of agreement as well as some of the main areas of disagreement.

- *A One-Volume Bible Commentary*

  It is helpful to have a good idea about what Christians may think of a verse before referring to it, and a one-volume Bible commentary gives a Christian interpretation of specific verses in the Bible. Probably the most widely recommended and used is *Matthew Henry's Commentary on the Whole Bible*, which is now available in one volume. This commentary, originally a five-volume work, has been influential for over two hundred years. There are many commentaries with many different opinions and they tend to be expensive acquisitions. For this type of information it is probably best to refer to a public library or some other source.

Such aids to studying the Bible and Christianity are effective and can make a working knowledge of *conservative* Christian beliefs more accessible for Bahá'ís.

SUGGESTIONS FOR EFFECTIVE BIBLE STUDY

Some Bahá'ís may think that studying the Bible requires too much effort, that the Bible is too difficult to read, and that the successful use of the technique described in this chapter will require too much memorization. To address this concern, *Preparing for a Bahá'í/Christian Dialogue* is designed to help readers retain and use what they learn from this study so that they can present it concisely to an inquirer and, in the end, converse persuasively with Christians. The following steps are suggested for organizing our study of the Bible and making it less difficult.

- We should begin by studying the New Testament. It is better to understand one book thoroughly – such as the Gospel of John – than to understand all of the books of the Bible superficially. It takes time to become familiar with the Bible, and embarking on a thorough study starting with Genesis will require a great deal of time before one even gets to the New Testament. Moreover, many people feel overwhelmed by the size of the Bible. Therefore, to make our study easier, most of the information in this book is selected from the New Testament. However, this is only a beginning. Such a study should eventually embrace the whole Bible.

• We should also become familiar with the order of the books in the Bible so that we can locate verses quickly and easily. A listing of the books of the Bible can be found in the table of contents at the beginning of any Bible. As an exercise, practice looking up Bible passages referred to in the Bahá'í writings. This will help to develop a sense of where to look without having to remember the sequence of the books each time. If no references are given for biblical verses in the Bahá'í text, use a Bible concordance to help locate the reference.

• When we create outlines in the Bible or our Bahá'í Books we should use abbreviations and keep notes. For example, we should mark the title and page number of the Bahá'í writings next to the passages in the Bible to which the writings apply or at the bottom of the same page. For example, write "KI 133" – representing "the *Kitáb-i-Íqán*, page 133" – next to Matthew 9:1–6. The Qur'ánic verse Bahá'u'lláh cites (KI 113) parallels Matthew 13:13. There are many more. This practice will help with locating Bahá'í commentary on biblical Scriptures.

• In addition to our basic color-code system using green, yellow, and blue markers, we can use a variety of colored pens or pencils to make notes in the margins of the Bible to indicate specific concepts, events, or persons. For example, a red line drawn vertically in the margin could indicate sections in the Gospels where people oppose Christ. We can then easily locate such passages and examine the reasons for opposition systematically. Using colored ink to record our study also facilitates easy reference in the future. With the same red-ink pen, we can mark all of the reasons Bahá'u'lláh sets out in the *Kitáb-i-Íqán* for the clergy's opposition to the Prophets.

We should write a question mark in the margin with a pencil (so that it can be erased later) when encountering passages that seem unclear. It may be helpful to make a list of such passages for the purpose of discussing them later with other interested or knowledgeable friends. It is important to mark verses as neatly as possible in the holy Scriptures, for they are sacred books and should be treated with reverence. We should also use a small ruler or straight edge when using the colored markers, and we should take care that the markers do not bleed through the paper.

- We should talk frequently with Christians, find other Bahá'ís who are interested in studying Christianity, and examine Christian literature. Also Christian radio and television broadcasts provide us with opportunities for learning about the beliefs and concerns of Christians.

Whole books have been written on effective methods for studying the Bible and are readily available at book stores, especially Christian book stores, and public libraries. It is beyond the scope of this book to present a comprehensive approach to studying the Bible; however, the steps mentioned above can serve as a point of departure for further explorations. Studying the Bible – like studying any other Scripture – is an ongoing process that promises many rewards.

The next chapter presents examples of how the information and methods we have learned can be applied.

6

DIALOGUES

ESTABLISHING BONDS OF FRIENDSHIP

Now that we have explored the concept of reasoning from Scripture, discussed the importance of acknowledging that the Bible is the Word of God, and learned some specific biblical criteria, we will look at some practical examples of how such criteria can be applied in discussions with Christians. First, we need to consider some basic points about establishing and maintaining bonds of agreement when we are trying to communicate with others.

Friendship, we all know, is usually characterized by some area of common agreement, shared belief, or mutual interest. Disagreements, on the other hand, quite often lead to antagonism and the loss of friendship. Sometimes a single point of contention can cause people to become so upset that they forget all they agree upon and share. Bahá'u'lláh counsels us to avoid such confrontations when we talk with others about what we believe:

Consort with all men, O people of Bahá, in a spirit of friendliness and fellowship. If ye be aware of a certain truth, if ye possess a jewel, of which others are deprived, share it with them in a language of utmost kindliness and good-will. If it be accepted, if it fulfill its purpose, your object is attained. If any one should refuse it, leave him unto himself, and beseech God to guide him. Beware lest ye deal unkindly with him. A kindly tongue is the lodestone of the hearts of men. It is the bread of the spirit, it clotheth the words with meaning, it is the fountain of the light of wisdom and understanding. (*Gleanings* 289)

As we have learned, we can help create and maintain a spirit of friendliness when discussing issues of faith and belief with people we meet by first establishing areas of common belief. But we must also learn how to keep that spirit of agreement at the forefront of our discussions. One way to accomplish this is to recognize when it is best to defer or de-emphasize issues of disagreement or potential disagreement. Whenever we see that the Bahá'í teachings are partly in agreement and partly in disagreement with the Christian's point of view, we have to make a decision as to whether to emphasize those points of agreement or disagreement.

'Abdu'l-Bahá encourages Bahá'ís to "first try and remove any apprehensions in the people they teach" (*Individual and Teaching* 12, No. 27). It is, therefore, better to discuss differences of belief *after* the bond of agreement has been established. In this way, we will start our discussions on friendly terms; and when differences arise, we will be able to examine them in an atmosphere of harmony, without arousing angry or hostile feelings. Generally, we will find it very difficult to remove people's apprehensions if we focus first on areas of disagreement.

We should also seek to avoid difficult theological issues that are likely to lead only to discord and arguments and, instead, focus on establishing the validity of Bahá'u'lláh's claims and teachings. If we enter into a controversial discussion, it is best to do so in an atmosphere of mutual inquiry and search, each participant asking questions and carefully considering every point. But not every situation will afford the opportunity to go into such detail.

The three hypothetical dialogues that follow in this chapter reflect such typical, limited circumstances. They are not complete or thorough examinations of any issue. They only begin to address a few of the ideas that are likely to enter a Bahá'í/Christian dialogue. However, they do provide examples of the different ways in which dialogues between Bahá'ís and Christians can be conducted, and they illustrate the underlying attitudes that can either help or hinder us in our conversations with Christians.

Each dialogue is followed by a critique. The first dialogue contains many errors. The second represents a somewhat more positive attempt to answer a Christian's questions. The third demonstrates the type of presentation that is the objective of this book.

DIALOGUE ONE: The ineffectiveness of a non-biblical approach

Let us suppose that a Bahá'í has just told a new acquaintance that she is a Bahá'í. She has shown the new acquaintance some Bahá'í literature and has mentioned some basic teachings of the Faith. She is hoping to open the dialogue further, but it goes badly, and the Christian goes away convinced that he is not interested in hearing anything more about the Bahá'í Faith:

Christian: What I hear sounds good to me, but I can't help wondering if this "Bahá'í Faith" isn't the kind of thing the Bible warns us about when it speaks of the Antichrist.

Bahá'í: Oh, no. Try to see the obvious logic and the world's need for the teachings of Bahá'u'lláh. I assure you, Bahá'u'lláh is not the Antichrist. Just about everyone in history has been accused of being the Antichrist. Who knows what the Bible really means. It has been translated so many times that its meaning has probably been changed considerably.

Christian: That sounds like the sort of thing the Devil wants us to believe. Personally, I believe the Bible is the Word of God and hasn't changed. Perhaps you should go back and read it a little more closely.

Bahá'í: As a Bahá'í, I don't believe in the Devil. The Devil represents our ego, and evil is simply the absence of good. The Devil is an outdated concept that was necessary in the past. But today, with the advent of modern psychology, we no longer need this concept.

Christian: Paul said, 'The wisdom of the world is foolishness with God.' Modern psychology is religion without God.

Bahá'í: I think we'd do better staying with the words of Christ. Paul never met Christ, and many scholars believe that Paul introduced a lot of ideas from the Greek mystery cults, which may be why the Church is so confused about the real message of Christ.

Christian: I don't mind staying with the words of Christ. Christ said, "I am the way, the truth, and the life. No one comes to the Father except through Me" (John 14:6). He also said, "For God so loved the world that He gave His only begotten Son, that whoever believes in Him should not perish but have everlasting life" (John 3:16). I suggest you read the Bible more carefully.

Bahá'í: Christ *was* the only way, but that was during His

era. This is a new day. We need to look at the
Bible symbolically and not so literally.

Christian: I hope the Lord will guide you to the truth. It's
been nice talking. I'll be praying for you.

The mistakes in this dialogue are numerous. Specifically, the
Bahá'í did not adequately listen to the Christian. This is
especially apparent in the way the Bahá'í failed to answer the
actual questions that the Christian asked. Unfortunately, she
also missed a good opportunity to examine biblical verses
about the Antichrist and then demonstrate that they do not
apply to Bahá'u'lláh.

The Bahá'í also failed to emphasize areas of agreement and
instead made some unfortunate assumptions about the accuracy of the translation and the authenticity of the verses in
question. For obvious reasons, such a negative approach to the
Bible aroused suspicions in the mind of the Christian. Alleging
that Christians have been or continue to be mistaken in their
interpretations of Scripture did not address the content of the
question. And, since most Christians do not regard the
Church's past mistakes as representative of contemporary
Christianity, the Bahá'í should have avoided such a dubious
approach.

Because the Bahá'í does not know how to use biblical
terminology, she also allowed herself to become sidetracked
by controversial issues such as the existence or non-existence
of evil and the Devil. Furthermore, she contributed to the
unproductive digression by needlessly trying to secularize
biblical terminology in offering her own interpretations, which
are at variance with the Bahá'í teachings.[27] The Bahá'í under-

---

27. 'Abdu'l-Bahá explains the Bahá'í concept of evil in chapters 57 and 74
of *Some Answered Questions* (212–16 and 263–4). In *Tablets of Bahá'u'lláh*,
Bahá'u'lláh uses phrases such as "the Evil One" (87), and "the foreboders of
evil" (123) and says "Indeed the actions of man himself breed a profusion of
satanic power" (176). At other times He clearly indicates that the real Satan
represents the selfish ego of man, as in His reference to the "Satan of self"

standing of the Devil is difficult to support effectively with the Bible because it involves allegorical interpretation. Because she had not yet established any areas of agreement with the Christian, the Bahá'í should have avoided subjects that she could not support directly with Scripture, and which are generally difficult to explain or are non-essential to the discussion.

Finally, the Bahá'í should have kept in mind that a Christian who presents verses that speak of Jesus as "the only way" is not being narrow-minded. Rather, such a Christian is using the Word of God to test a challenging issue – the Bahá'í Faith. A Bahá'í presented with such a challenge will very likely respond in the same way by examining it in the light of Bahá'í teachings. Had the Bahá'í confirmed the Bible's truth and examined verses such as John 14:6, she would have had little difficulty in continuing the dialogue. In this dialogue we have seen that the Bahá'í failed to follow any of the three essential steps: listening, emphasizing areas of agreement, and adapting the presentation to the audience.

DIALOGUE TWO: Missing a good opportunity through lack of evidence

This dialogue begins under the same circumstances as Dialogue One.

Christian: What I hear sounds good to me, but I can't help wondering if this 'Bahá'u'lláh' isn't the Antichrist mentioned in the Bible.

(*Kitáb-i-Íqán* 112) and in the following statement : "They say: 'Where is Paradise, and where is Hell?' Say: 'The one is reunion with Me; the other thine own self" (*Tablets of Bahá'u'lláh* 118). The Guardian writes: "We know absence of light is darkness, but no one would assert darkness was not a fact. It exists even though it is only the absence of something else. So evil exists too, and we cannot close our eyes to it, even though it is a negative existence (*Unfolding Destiny* 458).

Bahá'í:　　　The Bible explains to us that the Antichrist is someone who rejects Jesus of Nazareth as the Messiah or Christ. Since Bahá'u'lláh teaches that Jesus was the Christ, it obviously doesn't apply.

Christian:　　Could you show me where it says that? I have always thought that the Antichrist will be someone who promises to bring about world unity and set up a global, totalitarian government.

Bahá'í:　　　Well, I'm not sure of exactly where it is in the Bible, but I know it's there.

For many Christians, if an argument can't be supported with verses from the Bible, there's no point in bringing it up, as the Bible is the standard that defines their beliefs. In this case, the Bahá'í knew the right answer but was unable to support it and, therefore, could not effectively dispel the Christian's apprehensions. A positive discussion might have followed had the Bahá'í supported her case with Scripture, but her inability to do so destroyed her credibility in the Christian's eyes. Such discussions usually end in frustration for both parties.

DIALOGUE THREE: The advantage of staying with the Scriptures

The same circumstances as before.

Christian:　　What you say sounds good to me, but perhaps Bahá'u'lláh is the Antichrist that the Bible warns us about.

Bahá'í:　　　If we turn to the Bible, as we should in such matters, our apprehensions will be dispelled. John explains that the Antichrist is anyone who denies that the historical Jesus was the actual Christ or

Messiah. John says, "and every spirit that does not confess that Jesus Christ has come in the flesh is not of God. And this is the spirit of the Antichrist" (1 John 4:3). John also tells us how to know the Spirit of God. He says "By this you know the Spirit of God: Every spirit that confesses that Jesus Christ has come in the flesh is of God" (1 John 4:2).

Christian: Does Bahá'u'lláh confess this?

Bahá'í: Yes. When we read the Bahá'í writings, it becomes evident that the Spirit of God is in Bahá'u'lláh. His teachings about Christ, speaking about the effect of Christ's crucifixion on humankind, say, "Know thou that when the Son of Man yielded up His breath to God, the whole creation wept with a great weeping. By sacrificing Himself, however, a fresh capacity was infused into all created things" (*Gleanings* 85). When we rely on the Bible, we are able to see with assurance that Bahá'u'lláh is of God.

Christian: But does Bahá'u'lláh say Jesus is Lord?

Bahá'í: Yes, Bahá'u'lláh says Jesus Christ is "Lord of the visible and invisible" (*Gleanings* 57). He also calls Him the "Lord of all being" (*Epistle* 100). And, as you are no doubt aware, Saint Paul says, "no one can say that Jesus is Lord except by the Holy Spirit" (1 Cor. 12:3). This verse assures us that Bahá'u'lláh is speaking by the Holy Spirit.

Christian: Even so, saying these kinds of things does not necessarily mean a person is a Prophet. After all, every Christian believes Jesus is Christ and Lord.

Bahá'í: That's true. But, since Jesus explained how we
               might know a true Prophet, we can rely on the
               Word of God rather than our own human stan-
               dards. He said, "You will know them by their
               fruits" (Matt. 7:16). That is, we will know a true
               Prophet by His teachings and His life.

Christian: But how do you know that is what is meant by
               fruits?

Bahá'í: Saint Paul explains the meaning of "fruits" in his
               Epistle to the Galatians. Paul says, "the fruit of
               the Spirit is love, joy, peace, long-suffering, kind-
               ness, goodness, faithfulness, gentleness, self-
               control" (Gal. 5:22–23). Furthermore, he says,
               "(for the fruit of the spirit is in all goodness, right-
               eousness, and truth), proving what is acceptable
               to the Lord" (Eph. 5:9–10). It's clear that, by
               "fruits," Christ means divine attributes and spiri-
               tual qualities. Everything in creation has its own
               qualities by which we recognize it. Christ is saying
               that we can recognize a true Prophet by these
               spiritual qualities.

Christian: But how do you know Bahá'u'lláh's teachings are
               all divine or from God? Satan has many ways of
               deceiving and misleading people. Perhaps it is
               only five percent evil, just enough to send you to
               hell.

Bahá'í: Christ assures us that we will be able to *know*
               them by their fruits, not that we will be unable to
               know them. Moveover, Christ says "A good tree
               cannot bear bad fruit, nor can a bad tree bear
               good fruit."

Christian: Where does Christ say that?

Bahá'í: In Matthew 7:18. You're right that we should be
             careful about being deceived, but remember,
             Christ said, we *will* know them by their fruits. If
             you want to make a decision about this, I think
             you should first become acquainted with
             Bahá'u'lláh's life and teachings. Then you will be
             better able to judge the truth of Bahá'u'lláh .

Christian: Well, it sounds important enough. Tell me more
             about Bahá'u'lláh so I'll know for myself.

By using the Bible, which is Scripture that the Christian
accepts and regards as authoritative, the Bahá'í demonstrated
important truths about Bahá'u'lláh. By quoting from memory
the Bahá'í showed her acceptance and reverence for the Bible.
Rather than rejecting Paul – as she did in the first dialogue –
the Bahá'í used Paul's writings to support her point and to
help the Christian better understand the meaning of Christ's
message.

Even though the Christian brought up the issues of the
Devil and evil, the Bahá'í did not allow herself to become
sidetracked by the terminology. Instead, she referred to the
Bible and kept the discussion on track. By using the Bible,
the Bahá'í assured the Christian that she, too, believes it to
be a standard for finding the truth. Also, the Bahá'í avoided
speculation that does not conform to the Bible's spiritual
text.

Using the Bible, quoting appropriate, memorized Scripture,
and avoiding fruitless speculation made Dialogue Three an
effective presentation. Even if the Bahá'í's assumptions about
the Scriptures she was quoting had turned out to be incorrect,
her method – relying on the Bible as much as possible – was
correct. Because the Bible is the Word of God, it logically
follows that its use will benefit us. Bahá'ís should, therefore,
have no inhibitions about teaching Christians. Even if our
efforts to teach the Bahá'í Faith by using biblical verses fail
to persuade those with whom we converse, we will leave a

positive impression of the Bahá'í attitude toward Christ and the Bible that reflects these words of Shoghi Effendi:

> As to the position of Christianity, let it be stated without any hesitation or equivocation that its divine origin is unconditionally acknowledged, that the Sonship and Divinity of Jesus Christ are fearlessly asserted, that the divine inspiration of the Gospel is fully recognized. (*Promised Day* 109)

In Part One we have learned steps for developing a spirit of friendliness and fellowship in our dialogues with Christians. Once we have established a positive spirit of communication, however, we may find that it is sometimes challenging to maintain. For example, we learned the importance of affirming that the Bible is the Word of God. This single point, unencumbered, is a clear area of agreement with conservative Christians. But reaching agreement on the intended meaning of the Bible is not always as easy. Many Christians accept the Bible as the Word of God, but they do not always agree, even among themselves, about the meaning of some passages or whole parts of the Bible. Such disagreements over the meaning of the Bible often arise because people use different approaches for the interpretation of Scripture.[28]

In many dialogues with Christians we will find that Bahá'ís interpret some passages of the Bible symbolically while Christians interpret them literally. If we are not careful, such differences can lead to disputes and undermine the positive spirit of the interactions we seek with Christians. The purpose of Part Two is to introduce us to the subject of interpretation. If we are convincing, the Christian or Christians with whom we speak may be willing to reconsider the merits of the interpretations they have learned and to examine and accept the Bahá'í point of view.

28. The study of the principles of interpretation is known as "hermeneutics". The actual interpretation of specific passages is referred to as "exegesis". See Harvey, *Handbook of Theological Terms* 90–1 and 117–18.

part two:

UNDERSTANDING SCRIPTURE

7

INTERPRETING SCRIPTURE

DISCERNING THE SPIRITUAL MEANING OF SCRIPTURE

In the Bible we find that Paul emphasizes that the meaning of Scripture should be spiritually discerned:

> These things we also speak, not in words which man's wisdom teaches but which the Holy Spirit teaches, comparing spiritual things with spiritual. But the natural man does not receive the things of the Spirit of God, for they are foolishness to him; nor can he know them, because they are spiritually discerned. (1 Cor. 2:13–14)

The Bahá'í teachings also advocate that when interpreting Scripture we should look for the spiritual meaning. 'Abdu'l-Bahá states:

> All the texts and teachings of the holy Testaments have intrinsic spiritual meanings. They are not to be taken literally. I, therefore, pray in your behalf that you may be given the power of understanding these inner real meanings of the Holy Scriptures and may become informed of the mysteries deposited in the words of the Bible so that

you may attain eternal life and that your hearts may be
attracted to the Kingdom of God. (*Promulgation* 459–60)

This statement requires careful analysis. Even though
'Abdu'l-Bahá states that all the texts have intrinsic spiritual
meanings and that they are not to be taken literally, this does
not mean that the texts never have literal meanings.

The word *They* in the second sentence refers to the intrinsic
spiritual meanings, not to *all* them. All the texts have spiritual
meanings, but not all them should be interpreted in an exclusively spiritual manner.[29]

Some of the verses in the Scriptures, those containing laws
for example, have an outward or literal meaning. We are told
in Exodus 20:13, "You shall not murder." This is quite literal.
But, even though it has a literal meaning, the significance and
reason for such a law involves an intrinsic spiritual meaning.
However, some verses or even whole passages in the Bible
have only spiritual meanings and should not be taken literally.
For example, Christ stated:

He who believes in Me, as the Scriptures has said, out of
his heart will flow rivers of living water. (John 7:38)[30]

This verse does not mean that if we believe in Christ, water
will literally pour out of our hearts. Christ is using a material
reality, 'living water', in a figurative way, that is, as a symbol or
metaphor to represent spiritual reality. In this case, living[31]

29. 'Abdu'l-Bahá interprets some passages in the Bible in away that
appears quite literal. For an example, see *Some Answered Questions* 108–9. In
Bahá'u'lláh's writings we also find instances of literal interpretations. See
Bahá'u'lláh, *Kitáb-i-Íqán* 62. Furthermore, Bahá'u'lláh interprets a whole
series of prophecies in a literal way to help support the truth of the Báb .
These Islamic prophecies can be found on pages 238–48 of the *Kitáb-i-Íqán*.

30. The King James Version reads, "out of his *belly* shall flow" (John
7:38).

31. According to Matthew Henry, the word *living* simply means moving.
In past times streams, rivers, and bodies of water that were in motion were
referred to as living (*Matthew Henry's Commentary* 1546).

water probably symbolizes the grace and comfort that comes from knowing the truth of Christ. It is the 'living water' that waters and nourishes the faith in us and those around us. But the meaning of this verse is not easily narrowed to a limited or singular meaning. Nevertheless, we can readily grasp the basic meaning by understanding the nature of the symbol 'living water'. Literal water brings life to the material world. Water satisfies the thirst of the body. Used in a spiritual context, the soul that thirsts finds satisfaction by obtaining the spiritual water of the Scriptures.

The example we have used (John 7:38) is understood by both Bahá'ís and conservative Christians to be symbolic and not literal. The spiritual meaning is easy to perceive, and the literal meaning appears untenable, for it serves no purpose and, in any event, it has never occurred. Thus, in some cases it is easy to justify a symbolic interpretation. In others we may not find it as easy to determine when a verse is symbolic. Furthermore, if we interpret a verse literally that is not intended to be understood in a literal sense, we will arrive at the wrong meaning, and the true meaning will remain concealed.

THE TWOFOLD LANGUAGE

To assist us in perceiving the inner meanings of Scripture, Bahá'u'lláh has explained that the Manifestations of God and the Apostles speak a twofold language: "It is evident unto thee that the Birds of Heaven and Doves of Eternity speak a twofold language." One language, Bahá'u'lláh explains, is "the outward language" which is "devoid of allusions ... unconcealed and unveiled." He states that the other language is "veiled and concealed" (*Kitáb-i-Íqán* 254–5).

There are many examples from Scripture that will demonstrate this concept. For example, regarding His Second Coming, Christ states that "of that day and hour no one knows" (Mark 13:32). Most Christian commentators understand this to mean that no one can say for certain when the Second Advent of Christ was to occur. The same meaning is also affirmed by Bahá'u'lláh (*Epistle* 143). Its meaning is therefore clear and unconcealed.

In another passage, also referring to His Second Coming, Christ states: "Immediately after the tribulation of those days the sun will be darkened, and the moon will not give its light; the stars will fall from heaven" (Matt. 24:29). In as much as Christians have widely disagreed about the meaning of this verse, its meaning is, in the words of Bahá'u'lláh, veiled and concealed. Its outward meaning appears impossible to accept unless we abandon the evidences of science. And even if a Christian acknowledges that the words are symbolic, it is not easy to determine what they symbolize with complete certainty.

Even when we are able to see the necessity of using symbols to explain spiritual truths,[32] we are still confronted with the question: Why don't the Scriptures indicate which passages are symbolic and which are to be interpreted literally? Earlier we referred to Jesus' words:

He who believes in Me, as the Scripture has said, out of his heart will flow rivers of living water. (John 7:38)

Jesus spoke these words but did not go on to explain the symbolism. Even though the next verse says, "He spoke concerning the Spirit," it does not say that living water is a symbol. Another example can be seen in this passage:

Then He [Jesus] said to another, "Follow Me." But he said, "Lord, let me first go and bury my father." Jesus said to him, "Let the dead bury their own dead" (Luke 9:59–60).

32. 'Abdu'l-Bahá explains why sumbols are necessary to illustrate spiritual and intellectual concepts in *Some Answered Questions*, ch. 16.

The Scriptures do not indicate that Jesus explained what He meant. We are left to assume that these words meant that the spiritually dead could bury the disciple's father while the disciple followed Jesus. This seems reasonable, for by using physical death as a symbol for disbelief, Jesus gives force to His words, emphasizing the loss and deprivation that comes from disbelief. However, He does not make this plain by expounding the meaning of the symbol. We are forced to think about His words in order to realize their significance for ourselves.

This example is not difficult to understand but, as we have already mentioned, sometimes symbolism can be more difficult to detect and understand. The story of Adam and Eve is one such instance. The Bible does not tell us that the story is symbolic. Whether we understand the story in a symbolic or literal way, we can see that the story is about the consequences of disobedience to God's command. The story has conveyed this and more for centuries. But in modern times scientific discoveries have lead many to conclude that the story cannot be a literal account of humankind's early beginnings. Some Christians have therefore concluded, and Bahá'ís agree, that the story is symbolic. By interpreting the story symbolically, many more meanings can be seen.[33]

Common sense tells us that when Jesus said, "Let the dead bury their own dead," He was not talking about dead people burying dead people. In the same way, some argue that common scientific knowledge indicates that the story about Adam and Eve is also symbolic. However, since the Bible does not state that the story is a symbol, many Christians continue to believe it is literally true. Similar disagreements arise over the interpretation of certain prophecies, miracles, and accounts of such events as Noah and the flood, and the Resurrection of Jesus. The Bahá'í writings explain why distinctions between what is symbolic and what is literal are left unclear in the Bible.

---

33. 'Abdu'l-Bahá explains some of the symbolic meanings of the account of Adam and Eve. See *Some Answered Questions*, ch. 30.

THE PURPOSE OF SYMBOLIC LANGUAGE

Bahá'u'lláh explains that the use of symbolic language has always been the method of God for distinguishing between "illumined hearts" and "barren soil":

> Know verily that the purpose underlying all these symbolic terms and abstruse allusions, which emanate from the Revealers of God's holy Cause, hath been to test and prove the peoples of the world; that thereby the earth of the pure and illuminated hearts may be known from the perishable and barren soil. From time immemorial such hath been the way of God amidst His creatures, and to this testify the records of the sacred books. (*Kitáb-i-Íqán* 49)

In another passage, Bahá'u'lláh further emphasizes that the "twofold language" exists for a purpose. The unconcealed language is to guide the seeker to truth, and the concealed language is meant to expose the malevolent.

> One language, the outward language, is devoid of allusions, is unconcealed and unveiled; that it may be a guiding lamp and a beaconing light whereby wayfarers may attain the heights of holiness, and seekers may advance into the realm of eternal reunion. ... The other language is veiled and concealed, so that whatever lieth hidden in the heart of the malevolent may be made manifest and their innermost being be disclosed. (*Kitáb-i-Íqán* 254–5)

Bahá'u'lláh explains that the leaders of religion attempt to justify their rejection of and opposition to the Prophets of God by insisting that such symbolic verses be fulfilled literally (see *Kitáb-i-Íqán* 80–2; 220). By this means such leaders hope to maintain their positions of authority over the people. They demand literal fulfillment of such verses rather than acknowledge the perfection and truth of the Manifestations of God. In this way such language discloses their malevolence.

Likewise, Jesus suggests that His purpose for using parables was not primarily to enlighten the unenlightened, but to harden the unbelief of the unbeliever (see Mark 4: 10–12, Matt.13:13). The author of Hebrews also asserts that there is a purpose in the way Scripture is written, i.e., to disclose the intentions of the heart:

> For the word of God *is* living and powerful, and sharper than any two-edged sword, piercing even to the division of soul and spirit, and of joints and marrow, and is a discerner of the thoughts and intents of the heart. (Heb. 4:12)

Notice how the spiritual terms "soul" and "spirit" are placed in relation to the physical terms "joints" and "marrow." The power of the Word of God separates like a two-edged sword cutting apart the sincere from the irreligious and self-righteous. This twofold language of the Word of God may be at the heart of Jesus' words: "Do not think that I came to bring peace on earth. I did not come to bring peace but a sword" (Matt. 10:34).[34]

Bahá'u'lláh uses "sword" to express the effect of the Word of God:

> How many fathers have turned away from their sons; how many lovers have shunned their beloved! So mercilessly trenchant was this wondrous sword of God that it cleft asunder every relationship! On the other hand, consider the welding power of His Word. Observe, how those in whose midst the Satan of self had for years sown the seeds

34. This interpretation of Matthew 10:34 is based on the author's understanding of 'Abdu'l-Bahá's talk given on 30 October 1911 entitled, "The True Meaning of the Prophecies Concerning the Coming of Christ" (see *Paris Talks* 54–7).

of malice and hate became so fused and blended through
their allegiance to this wondrous and transcendent Revelation that it seemed as if they had sprung from the same
loins. (*Kitáb-i-Íqán* 112)

The term "sword" is a natural metaphor for the Word of God
because the Word of God separates the "illumined hearts"
from the "barren soil."

To understand the purpose of the twofold language, we
need to keep in mind that the decision of faith rests upon the
exercise of our free will. Bahá'u'lláh points out that if the
prophecies were fulfilled literally rather than symbolically, the
fulfillment would be so startling as to cause everyone to believe
and, therefore, would interfere with the exercise of our free
will:

As the adherents of Jesus have never understood the
hidden meaning of these words, and as the signs which
they and the leaders of their Faith have expected have
failed to appear, they therefore refused to acknowledge,
even until now, the truth of those Manifestations of
Holiness that have since the days of Jesus been made
manifest. ... They have even failed to perceive that were
the signs of the Manifestation of God in every age to
appear in the visible realm in accordance with the text of
established traditions, none could possibly deny or turn
away, nor would the blessed be distinguished from the
miserable, and the transgressor from the God-fearing.
Judge fairly: Were the prophecies recorded in the Gospel to be literally fulfilled; were Jesus, Son of Mary,
accompanied by angels to descend from the visible
heaven upon the clouds; who would dare to disbelieve,
who would dare reject the truth, and wax disdainful? Nay,
such consternation would immediately seize all the dwell-
ers of the earth that no soul would feel able to utter a
word, much less to reject or accept the truth. (*Kitáb-i-
Íqán* 80–1)

Allusions to the purpose behind the words of Scripture are also apparent in the teachings of Christ. In the Gospel of Matthew it is written:

> Therefore I speak to them in parables, because seeing they do not see, and hearing they do not hear, nor do they understand. And in them the prophecy of Isaiah is fulfilled, which says:
>
> > *'Hearing you will hear and shall not understand,*
> > *And seeing you will see and not perceive;*
> > *For the heart of this people has grown dull,*
> > *Their ears are hard of hearing,*
> > *And their eyes they have closed,*
> > *Lest they should see with their eyes and hear with their ears,*
> > *Lest they should understand with their heart and turn,*
> > *So that I should heal them'*
> > But blessed are your eyes for they see, and your ears for they hear (Matt. 13:13–16).

Christ states that He speaks in parables so that the spiritually minded and those who seek diligently will discover His meaning, but those who are neither receptive nor seeking spiritual knowledge will not appreciate the significance of His teachings.[35]

PREREQUISITES FOR UNDERSTANDING SCRIPTURE

Even though the holy Books contain symbolic terms, hidden meanings and allegories, they are not incomprehensible or beyond the reach of those who are willing to be open minded and look for their spiritual meanings. When Paul stated that the Scriptures "are spiritually discerned"

---

35. The prophecy of Isaiah to which Christ refers here is Isaiah 6:9–10 and is frequently referred to in the New Testament. See Matt. 13:15; Luke 8:10; John 12:40; Acts 28:26–7; Rom. 10:16,11:8.

(1 Cor. 2:14), he was pointing out that, because of the spiritual nature of the Scriptures, they must be understood from a spiritual point of view. To understand Scripture, one must be detached and spiritually oriented. In other words, the prerequisites for understanding the Scriptures are spiritual qualities.

Bahá'u'lláh assures us that God "hath endowed every soul with the capacity to recognize the signs of God" (*Gleanings* 105–6). However, these capacities can become obscured by worldliness or human limitations. Throughout the *Kitáb-i-Íqán* Bahá'u'lláh stressed the importance of detachment as an essential prerequisite to true understanding:

> they that tread the path of faith, they that thirst for the wine of certitude, must cleanse themselves of all that is earthly – their ears from idle talk, their minds from vain imaginings, their hearts from worldly affections, their eyes from that which perisheth. (*Kitáb-i-Íqán* 3)

In an other passage Bahá'u'lláh continues this theme:

> Wert thou to cleanse the mirror of thy heart from the dust of malice, thou wouldst apprehend the meaning of the symbolic terms revealed by the all-embracing Word of God made manifest in every Dispensation, and wouldst discover the mysteries of divine knowledge. Not, however, until thou consumest with the flame of utter detachment those veils of idle learning, that are current amongst men, canst thou behold the resplendent morn of true knowledge. (*Kitáb-i-Íqán* 68–9)

Bahá'u'lláh rejects the idea that only a scholar can understand Scripture:

> The understanding of His words and the comprehension of the utterances of the Birds of Heaven are in no wise dependent upon human learning. They depend solely

upon purity of heart, chastity of soul, and freedom of spirit. (*Kitáb-i-Íqán* 211)

Many religious leaders undergo years of extensive training and are often very learned. However, Bahá'u'lláh informs us that sometimes the leaders of religion fail to perceive the truth because they become attached to their own concepts and positions of leadership:

> These leaders, owing to their immersion in selfish desires, and their pursuit of transitory and sordid things, have regarded these divine Luminaries as being opposed to the standards of their knowledge and understanding, and the opponents of their ways and judgments. As they have literally interpreted the Word of God, and the sayings and traditions of the Letters of Unity, and expounded them according to their own deficient understanding, they have therefore deprived themselves and all their people of the bountiful showers of the grace and mercies of God. (*Kitáb-i-Íqán* 82)

These passages from Bahá'u'lláh's writings emphasize the importance of investigating the truth for ourselves and studying the Scriptures on our own.

THE KEY THAT UNLOCKS THE SYMBOLIC MESSAGE OF THE SCRIPTURES

The Book that will help us most in our efforts to understand Scripture is the *Kitáb-i-Íqán*. This Book provides general guidelines for interpreting Scriptures and specifically explains many issues that will help us discuss the Bible with Christians.

Because the *Kitáb-i-Íqán* is addressed to an Islamic audience, some may assume it has little application to Christian issues. But close examination yields a completely different understanding. Large portions of the text actually elucidate the meaning of passages from the New Testament. Even beyond such an obvious indication of the *Kitáb-i-Íqán's* relevance to Christian topics, most of its contents are closely related to important Christian questions and issues. Although the *Kitáb-i-Íqán* was written in answer to certain questions which reflect an Islamic point of view, they are nevertheless very similar to questions of concern to many Christians. These questions can be summarized briefly as follows:

- **The Day of Resurrection** – Is there to be physical resurrection? How are the just to be rewarded and the unjust to be punished?

- **The Twelfth Imám**[36] – According to Muslim traditions, He was born at a given time in history yet He lives on. How can such a phenomenon be explained?

- **Interpretation of Holy Texts** – The Bahá'í Faith does not seem to endorse the literal meanings of Scripture held throughout the centuries. How can the new interpretations be explained?

- **Advent of the Qá'im**[37] – Certain events, according to the traditions that have come down from the Imáms, must occur at the advent of the Qá'im. But none of these have happened. How can the absence of promised signs be explained?[38]

---

36. The term "Twelfth Imám" refers to the Promised One or Messiah of Shi'ah Islam Who is expected to reappear on Judgment Day. Bahá'ís regard the Báb as the fulfillment of this expectation.

37. "Qá'im" is another title for the Promised One of Islám.

38. This list of Muslim concerns is based on the list in Balyuzi, *Bahá'u'lláh: The King of Glory* 164–5.

The following Christian questions offer clear parallels to the Islamic questions:

- **The Day of Resurrection** – In Paul's description of the Second Coming of Christ, he wrote: "Then we who are alive *and* remain shall be caught up together with them in the clouds to meet the Lord in the air" (1 Thess. 4:17). This event is commonly referred to as the 'rapture' or 'translation' of the church. Is this event to take place physically? How is the 'judgment' foretold in Scripture (Rev. 20:12–13) going to take place? If the 'end' (Matt. 24:14) has already come, where is the 'judgment' (2 Pet. 2:9, Isa. 2:4)?

- **The Return** – The New Testament proclaims that Jesus rose from the dead on the third day after His crucifixion (Matt. 28, Mark 16, Luke 24, John 20). Many Christians believe that Jesus conquered physical death and lives on. Yet the Bahá'í Faith teaches that the resurrection of Christ has a spiritual significance and was not a physical event. How is this view explained?

- **The Interpretation of the Holy Books** – Many passages in the Bible have been traditionally interpreted to have literal meanings such as the prophecies in Matthew ch. 24. The Bahá'í Faith teaches that such verses were intended to be interpreted symbolically. How can this be explained?

- **Prophecies and Signs** – Certain events, according to the Scriptures, must occur at the time of the Return of Christ: the sun will be darkened, the moon will fall from heaven (Matt. 24:29). Apparently none of these events have happened. If Bahá'u'lláh is the Promised One, how can the absence of such dramatic occurrences be explained?

In each case there is a Christian equivalent to the Islamic question, all of which are central to Christian doctrine and thought. Moreover, these issues are likely to arise often in conversations with conservative Christians. Although the interpretation of Scripture is treated separately from the other questions in the list, the answers to all of these questions will depend on how the Scriptures are interpreted and understood.

Not all these questions will be important to every Christian, nor will they be the only ones Christians will ask. However, the broad range of the *Kitáb-i-Íqán* will help us address any difficulty we are likely to encounter in a Bahá'í/Christian dialogue. The Guardian wrote:

> Well may it be claimed that of all the books revealed by the Author of the Bahá'í Revelation, this Book alone [the *Kitáb-i-Íqán*], by sweeping away the age-long barriers that have so insurmountably separated the great religions of the world, has laid down a broad and unassailable foundation for the complete and permanent reconciliation of their followers. (*God Passes By* 139)

Bahá'u'lláh assures us that an understanding of the *Kitáb-i-Íqán* is a means by which we can overcome the barriers that hinder people from recognizing the Promised One:

> Wert thou to heed these words, wert thou to ponder their outward and inner meaning in thy heart, thou wouldst seize the significance of all the abstruse problems which, in this day, have become insuperable barriers between men and the knowledge of the Day of Judgment. Then wilt thou have no more questions to perplex thee. (*Kitáb-i-Íqán* 123)

Bahá'u'lláh, again expressing the broad and comprehensive nature of the *Kitáb-i-Íqán*, writes:

all the Scriptures and the mysteries thereof are condensed into this brief account. (*Kitáb-i-Íqán* 237)

Furthermore, the *Kitáb-i-Íqán* is a foundation on which an understanding of all the difficult issues of past revelations can be built. For example, some people find statements in the Scriptures that they believe are errors or contradictions, and their faith begins to falter. A thorough knowledge of the *Kitáb-i-Íqán's* contents provides a safe means for resolving such issues with steadfast faith. Bahá'u'lláh writes:

> All these things which We have repeatedly mentioned, and the details which We have cited from divers sources, have no other purpose but to enable thee to grasp the meaning of the allusions in the utterances of the chosen Ones of God, lest certain of these utterances cause thy feet to falter and thy heart to be dismayed. (*Kitáb-i-Íqán* 134)

SUMMARY

The key points we have covered concerning interpretation consist of the following: Both the Bahá'í writings and the Bible indicate that the Scriptures are to be understood primarily in a spiritual rather than literal manner. Although certain scriptural texts have an important literal meaning, the texts contain concealed meanings for a purpose: to distinguish between the pure in heart and the worldly minded. These concealed meanings can be perceived and understood by those who detach and sanctify themselves from imitation and worldly desires. This detachment and an awareness of Scripture's purpose constitute the essential prerequisites for the interpretation of Scripture. The next chapter will consider the Christian argument for interpreting the Bible literally.

8

RESPONDING TO ARGUMENTS FOR LITERAL INTERPRETATION

THE CHRISTIAN ARGUMENT FOR THE LITERAL INTERPRETATION OF THE BIBLE

In preparation for discussions on the interpretation of the Bible it is important to consider some of the arguments used by Christians to support and justify a literal interpretation. Literalists do not deny that the Scriptures contain symbols, metaphors, analogies, and figurative language, even as Bahá'ís do not deny that some verses have literal meanings. The issue is rather the extent to which literalism is applied.

Literalists assume that most Scripture is intended to be taken literally and that exceptions should be made only when specifically indicated by the text itself. They argue that God desires for humankind to understand His message, therefore He chose to convey it in clear and ordinary human language. They believe that the assertion that Scripture contains hidden meanings contradicts God's desire to have His words understood. Moreover, they object to symbolic and allegorical interpretation because they believe it gives rise to a multiplicity of meanings that, in turn, lead to confusion.

Since humankind is finite, literalists believe God uses a finite language with finite meanings so that humankind can comprehend it. Because literalists believe Scripture is written in ordinary language, it follows from their point of view that it should be interpreted only by regular rules of grammar and rhetoric and in accordance with the historical context of its use.

Some will even argue that it is irreverent to assume Scripture has hidden meanings because this implies God could not convey through the Scriptures, in a straightforward manner, all that He wanted humankind to know. Since, in an actual situation, they argue, a speaker intends only one meaning by his or her words, the Bible must also primarily intend only one meaning.[39]

RESPONDING TO CHRISTIAN ARGUMENTS

The Christian arguments we have considered rest on the assumption that literal interpretation of Scripture makes Scripture comprehensible, easily understandable, and less confusing. From a rational point of view, the arguments fail to persuade because literalism does not yield conclusions comprehensible to those who give weight to scientific conclusions. Examples of this will be cited later. From a historical point of view, the divisions among literalists make it evident that they do not agree even among themselves on the meaning of Scripture. Like those who interpret Scripture symbolically, literalists also arrive at differing points of view, thus giving rise to a multiplicity of meanings.

Such a multiplicity of meaning is not inherently confusing unless each proponent asserts that his or her view is the only correct view. Bahá'u'lláh writes:

in the sayings of Him Who is the Spirit (Jesus) unnumbered significances lie concealed. (Epistle 148)

39. See Paul Lee Tan, *The Interpretation of Prophecy* 61–2.

and:

> Know assuredly that just as thou firmly believest that the
> Word of God, exalted be His glory, endureth forever,
> thou must, likewise, believe with undoubting faith that its
> meaning can never be exhausted. (*Gleanings* 175)

This understanding demands tolerance on the part of every
believer when making interpretations and listening to another's point of view. Both the Bible and the Bahá'í writings
assert that God uses the spiritual or symbolic language of
Scripture to test His servants not to confuse them or keep
them from understanding. God has both given Scripture hidden meanings and endowed human beings with the capacity to
perceive and understand Scripture.

Literalism and the words of Jesus

To support the Bahá'í method of interpretation we can turn to
the Bible for examples. It can be shown that literalism during
the ministry of Jesus often blinded people to the real meanings
of Jesus' words.

Jesus often spoke in parables, a form of concise, simple
stories, to convey spiritual lessons. There are also many
instances where Jesus used words in a symbolic manner
without the use of a story (i.e., a parable) to illustrate His
points. Specific examples can be seen in Jesus' teachings about
being "born again" and His being "the bread from heaven." In
each example, those listening to Jesus misunderstood His
words because they interpreted His sayings literally and did
not see that He was explaining spiritual truths through symbols.

When Jesus said:

> Most assuredly, I say to you unless one is born again, he
> cannot see the kingdom of God. (John 3:3)

Nicodemus responded by saying:

> How can a man be born when he is old? Can he enter a
> second time into his mother's womb and be born? (John
> 3:4)

The following is another similar example. Jesus said:

> I am the living bread which came down from heaven. If
> anyone eats of this bread, he will live forever; and the
> bread that I shall give is My flesh, which I shall give for the
> life of the world. (John 6:51)

Consider the response to Jesus' words. The Gospel records:

> The Jews therefore quarreled among themselves, saying,
> "How can this *Man* give us *His* flesh to eat?" (John 6:52)

Even His followers failed to understand and said:

> This is a hard saying; who can understand it? (John 6:60)

Jesus then indicated that His discourse was to be understood
spiritually with these words:

> It is the Spirit who gives life; the flesh profits nothing. The
> words that I speak to you are spirit, and *they* are life. (John
> 6:63)

Nevertheless, the Gospel tells us that many stopped following
Christ because of these teachings (John 6:66). This indicates
that Christ clearly used words in a symbolic manner, even to
the extent that people turned away without having understood. Such examples present a clear challenge to literalists
who argue that the Bible uses ordinary common language so
humankind can understand God's teachings. However, when
we discuss this issue with Christians, we should not confuse

the parables that Jesus related with other types of symbols such as "being born again" or "the bread from heaven."

Throughout the Gospel, Jesus usually expounded His messages by telling short stories that used common circumstances in allegorical ways to illustrate spiritual truths. In some cases we find that Jesus provides explanations, such as for the parables of the sower and the tares (Matt. 13:18–23, 36–43), and the dragnet (Matt. 13:47–50). Others, such as the wicked husbandmen (Mark 12:1–12), the marriage feast (Matt. 22:1–14), and the great supper (Luke 14:16–24), are not given detailed explanations, and the hearers were left to make their own conclusions. Even though the meaning of each parable is concealed in the symbol that the parable uses, in most cases the symbol is not difficult to understand.

Most Christians readily acknowledge that Jesus used symbols when He spoke in parables. However, for Christians, this does not justify the belief that other parts of the Gospel are also symbolic. We should understand that parables are therefore not sufficient evidence that the Bible should primarily be interpreted in a symbolic way. Nevertheless, from the Bahá'í point of view, the parables are a clear indication that Jesus used symbols to explain spiritual realities.

Saint Paul's allegorical interpretations

The letters of Paul also provide biblical evidence for the Bahá'í approach to interpretation. Paul's writings contain instances of allegorical interpretation of the Old Testament, which affirm that Scripture can have multiple meanings – spiritual meanings which are not evident if interpreted literally.[40]

40. The early Church fathers, most notably Justin Martyr, Clement of Alexandria, and Origen, believed that Paul's use of allegory validated the allegorical method of interpretation. The Church fathers borrowed both from the Jewish method of nonliteral interpretation described as "midrash" and the Greek method termed "allegoria." See Wolfson's *The Philosophy of the Church Fathers*, ch. 2: 24–72.

Although Paul does not deny an actual historcal reality for the accounts, he nevertheless arrives at conclusions which are not apparent in the literal sense:

> For it is written that Abraham had two sons: the one by a bondwoman, the other by a freewoman. But he who was of the bondwoman was born according to the flesh, and he of the freewoman through promise, which things are symbolic. For these are the two covenants: the one from Mount Sinai which gives birth to bondage, which is Hagar – for this Hagar is Mount Sinai in Arabia, and corresponds to Jerusalem which now is, and is in bondage with her children – but the Jerusalem above is free, which is the mother of us all. (Gal. 4:22–6)

This interpretation by Paul is based on Genesis, ch. 13. Paul explains that Sarai's maidservant Hagar is a symbol of Mount Sinai in Arabia, which he says represents Jerusalem. In Paul's day Jerusalem was under Roman domination. Paul uses this domination, or bondage, metaphorically to express the bondage of the Jews to the law of Moses. Thus, Paul sees Hagar as a symbol of Jerusalem because Hagar was a bondwoman, and Jerusalem was under Roman bondage. Clearly, in Sarai, Hagar, Mount Sinai and Jerusalem, Paul perceived symbolic meanings that are not apparent in the literal sense of Genesis, ch. 13.

In another example it is recorded:

> "Behold, I will stand before you there on the rock in Horeb; and you shall strike the rock, and water will come out of it, that the people may drink." And Moses did so in the sight of the elders of Israel. (Exod. 17:6)

Paul does not interpret this passage literally as water running out of a rock. Instead he writes:

> Moreover, brethren, I do not want you to be unaware that all our fathers were under the cloud, all passed through

the sea, all were baptized into Moses in the cloud and in the sea, all ate the same spiritual food, and all drank the same spiritual drink. For they drank of that spiritual Rock that followed them, and that Rock was Christ. (1 Cor. 10:1–4)

Paul sees Christ pre-figured in this account of Exodus, even though the author of Exodus did not give any indication that such passages are symbolic and are not intended to be understood in an exclusively literal sense.

Again in Exodus we find another apparently literal historical event, which Paul interprets symbolically. It is recorded that, after Moses spoke with God, his face shone so brightly the people of Israel were afraid to come near Him. This caused Moses to veil his face when He spoke to the Israelites (Exod. 34). Paul interprets this account in Exodus allegorically, explaining why the Jews do not understand the Scriptures as the Christians do:

Therefore, since we have such hope, we use great boldness of speech – unlike Moses, *who* put a veil over his face so that the children of Israel could not look steadily at the end of what was passing away. But their minds were hardened. For until this day the same veil remains unlifted in the reading of the Old Testament, because the *veil* is taken away in Christ. But even to this day, when Moses is read, a veil lies on their heart. Nevertheless when one turns to the Lord, the veil is taken away. (2 Cor. 3:12–16)

In this case Paul sees the veil over Moses' face as a symbol of the Jews' non-acceptance of Christ and, consequently, their inability to understand the real message of the Scriptures. In each of these examples Paul goes beyond the literal meaning and reveals a hidden spiritual meaning. Yet there is no indication in the text that these passages have any intended meanings other than in the literal sense. Paul must have believed that Scripture contains concealed meanings even in instances when it appears to be quite literal.

How some literalists grapple with Paul

Christians are not unaware of these examples, and some advocates of the literal approach have therefore resorted to a variety of arguments to defuse Paul's use of allegorical interpretation. One argument is that Paul only used the method because the Jews to whom he wrote respected such an approach, not because he believed it was valid. Such an idea is ironic, as the Scriptures give no indication that Paul used allegory just for argument's sake, and literalists purport to accept the plain meaning of Scripture unless specifically indicated otherwise.

Another argument asserts that Paul is reflecting a flawed type of interpretation, which he learned as a student of Gamaliel (Acts 22:3). It assumes that Paul is wrong and that he is imitating methods of interpretation which are allegedly erroneous. Such arguments are clearly based on conjecture, not on biblical evidence.

A point should be noted here regarding Paul's interpretations: He never directly denies the historical or literal sense when he gives his interpretations. Therefore, these examples from the letters of Paul cannot be used to demonstrate that passages and verses which Bahá'ís believe to be symbolic do not also have actual literal meanings as well. These examples indicate that the text can be symbolic even when no indication of symbolism is given, that the Scriptures have more than one meaning, and that these meanings are concealed or not evident in the literal sense indicated by the words.

The role of contemporary science and reason

One of the main reasons why the Bahá'í Faith interprets much of the Bible symbolically stems from the value placed on reason and the validity of modern scientific knowledge. Christians who hold to traditional literal interpretations often find their beliefs in conflict with the evidence of modern science. As a result, some Christians re-interpret the Bible in the light of modern knowledge, but others feel that it is safer to follow tradition. The Bahá'í Faith teaches that religion must be reasonable. Thus when an interpretation is untenable in the face of sound scientific understanding, that interpretation must be re-evaluated.

The Bahá'í view holds that the faculty of the intellect and reason is the "supreme emblem of God" (*Secret of Divine Civilization* 1) and, therefore, should be used in the study of religion (*Paris Talks* 144). This belief can be seen in the fact that many of 'Abdu'l-Bahá's explanations of the holy Books reflect contemporary scientific thought. For example, consider 'Abdu'l-Bahá's explanation of a prophecy from Matthew, ch. 24:

> Among other things it is said that the stars will fall upon the earth. The stars are endless and innumerable, and modern mathematicians have established and proved scientifically that the globe of the sun is estimated to be about one million and a half times greater than the earth, and each of the fixed stars to be a thousand times larger than the sun. If these stars were to fall upon the surface of the earth, how could they find place there? It would be as though a thousand million of Himalaya mountains were to fall upon a grain of mustard seed. According to reason and science this thing is quite impossible. (*Some Answered Questions* 111–12)

'Abdu'l-Bahá does not reject the prophecy as untrue or dispute that it is the Word of God; rather He rejects that it should be interpreted literally. It is evident that the Bahá'í view values proven scientific knowledge as a factor to be considered when interpreting Scripture.

Some Christians who hold to the literal view reject this approach. They argue that the Bible contains many instances when God clearly intervened in the laws of nature to enforce His will. For example, God enabled Moses to part the sea. It is not scientifically possible that a human being could have such power, but God gave Moses the power. In the same way, God can alter aspects of the natural universe, such as the size of the stars, to fulfill the prophecies of Scripture in a literal way. Using this type of reasoning, modern science does not become a significant factor for some literalists when they interpret the Bible.

The Bahá'í Faith agrees that God is all powerful and can do as He wills, but there is no clear evidence in the Bible that God has changed natural laws in a radical way in the past and will therefore do so in the future. The literalists assume that by literally interpreting portions of the Bible, such as in the case of the parting of the sea, they can find evidence to support the view that God does disrupt the natural laws of the universe to accomplish His will. With this evidence they seek to support literal interpretations of prophecy that suggest God will interfere in natural laws in the future.

This evidence is not persuasive if we acknowledge that much of the Old Testament may also be symbolic. In other words, literal interpretations are not sufficient evidence to justify more literal interpretation. Many of the episodes recorded in the Old Testament appear to be actual history, well supported by archaeological evidence, but whether all of it actually occurred literally is at present impossible to determine. This is especially true with regard to miraculous events. The Bible brings together both symbol and the narrative of actual history to convey spiritual truths. In this way the Prophets and writers of the Bible breathed the inspiration of God into their accounts. The Bahá'í approach relies on reason to help us ascertain which parts are symbolic and what they symbolize. It is important to understand that symbolism is not a distortion of the facts, it is a device used to convey the spiritual significance of events that we would otherwise fail to appreciate.

Some extreme advocates of literalism, in their efforts to reconcile contradictions between their beliefs and the laws of nature, even assert that discoveries that conflict with their literal interpretations of the Bible are deceptions of Satan. Christians who hold such views often regard scientific knowledge as evil.

When speaking with Christians who have very negative views about science, it may be best to avoid directly addressing this issue. There are positive points we could bring up, such as examples of how science has helped the spread of the Bible around the world, enabled researchers to discover ancient evidence supporting the truth of the Bible, and provided tests for dating biblical texts. But when such Christians assume anything contradicting their understanding of the Bible to be part of a plot by Satan to subvert their faith in Christ, it is especially important to avoid arguments that go beyond the immediate text of the Bible. When we come to verses which Bahá'ís and Christians interpret differently, rather than argue about the meaning we should move on, looking for points of agreement and working from there.

INTERPRETATION IS A COMPLEX ISSUE

It must be pointed out that the subject of interpretation is extremely complex and multi-faceted. The issues we touched on in these two chapters serve only to introduce the very basic foundation points. These points will help us as we begin our study of Scripture. However, since this book cannot cover every aspect of the subject or provide interpretations of all the Scriptures, the importance of studying the *Kitáb-i-Íqán* cannot be overstated. That Book shows us how to interpret Scripture in a way that is spiritual and well reasoned, and thus a careful examination of its contents is of great relevance to our preparations for a Bahá'í/Christian dialogue.

BIBLICAL REFERENCES

The following verses are from this chapter about interpretation and can be used to form an outline in the back of our Bible. This referencing procedure was described in Chapter 5. Use a yellow marker to highlight the following verses:

The interpretation of Scripture:

Purpose of spiritual language of Scripture: Matt. 13:13–16, Heb. 4:12

Scripture is spiritually discerned: 1 Cor. 2:13–14

Literalists misunderstood symbols of Jesus: John 3:3–4, 6:51–66

Paul interprets Scripture allegorically: Gal. 4:22–6, 1 Cor. 10:1–4, 2 Cor. 3:12–16. (It is also recommended that we note in the margin, if it is not already printed in our Bible, the corresponding verses in the Old Testament that Paul is interpreting: Gen. 16:15, 17:19–20, 21:2; Exod. 17:6, 34:29–35.)

part   three:

PROOFS

HOW TO DEMONSTRATE THAT BAHÁ'U'LLÁH IS A MANIFESTATION OF GOD

THE PROOF OF BAHÁ'U'LLÁH'S CLAIMS

The subject of Part Three contains the most important information we will examine – the evidence supporting the truth of Bahá'u'lláh's claims. It is important because many people will feel that the Bahá'í Faith does not warrant investigation if Bahá'ís are unable to answer the question: How do we *know* Bahá'u'lláh is who He claimed to be? We must, therefore, be able to explain in the form of rational arguments that we know Bahá'u'lláh is a Manifestation of God because in His life and teachings we can perceive the divine reality of God's attributes. Moreover, we can personally experience and know for ourselves the reality of these divine attributes by practicing His teachings in our own lives and coming to know God through the person of Bahá'u'lláh.

Many people fail to perceive the proof of Bahá'u'lláh's claims because they are unaware of what constitutes appropriate evidence and/or have the wrong expectations. For example, when Jesus was on the cross, the people watching Him mockingly said, "He saves others; Himself He cannot save. If He is the King of Israel, let Him now come down from the cross, and we will believe Him" (Matt. 27:42). These people awaited a Messiah who they believed would be a king and who would liberate them from the Romans; hence, for them, proof of Jesus' Lordship, that He was indeed King, consisted of whether or not He had the power to free Himself from the cross. Jesus, however, did not provide this proof because the real proof of Jesus' power lay in His ability to free those who accepted Him from real bondage – not the bondage of Rome, but of sin. Moreover, He willingly died on the cross as an evidence of His love for humankind, that it might awaken us to the depth of His relationship to God and the truth of His experience. Through this example and His teachings, He transformed people's lives and established His real Lordship. His sacrifice testified that it was not winning a military battle against Rome, as the Jews expected, that leads to the Kingdom of God, but winning the spiritual battle.

Even as Christ's power was revealed through His triumph over the cross, Bahá'u'lláh's power and glory are revealed through His triumph over His exiles and imprisonments. Yet, today, many Christians are expecting Christ to literally return in the clouds of heaven, and with great power He is to conquer all the peoples of the world who rise up against Him. Following His glorious victory, He is then expected to establish the Kingdom of God on earth for those who believe in Him. Therefore, to Christians, Bahá'u'lláh's exiles and imprisonments are often seen as having no relationship to the Bible and as an indication of weakness, just as the Jews perceive Jesus' death on the cross. Yet the reality of Bahá'u'lláh has come from God's heaven and all the opposition that Bahá'u'lláh was subjected to has failed to stop the triumph of His Word over the hearts of those who believe in Him. He is, in fact, conquering the world through the spiritual transformation He is bringing about within all the people who have received Him and, in this way, is establishing the Kingdom of God in the hearts of humankind. This is the real victory of the returned Christ, the real meaning of power and glory, and it is this victory that is the evidence and proof of Bahá'u'lláh's claims! It is, moreover, an evidence that we can experience as believers.

Bahá'u'lláh says, "We, verily, have come for your sakes, and have borne the misfortunes of the world for your salvation"

(*Tablet of Bahá'u'lláh* 10). In this verse Bahá'u'lláh links His ministry of sacrifice directly to our personal salvation. It is extremely important for us to realize this on a personal level and to be able to convey it to Christians, as well as to the rest of the world. If we do not convey the significance of Bahá'u'lláh, the Bahá'í Faith will appear to Christians to be no more than a secular ideology or philosophy, and not what it is – a relationship to God established through the sacrificial ministry of Bahá'u'lláh and experienced in the heart of every believer.

The evidence of Bahá'u'lláh's truth stands on its own spiritual merits whether we are relating it to the Bible while speaking with a Christian or conveying it without reference to the Bible to non-Christians. Nevertheless, because the objective of this book is to help Bahá'ís convey this evidence to Christians, we will examine how this understanding can be presented to them from the stand point of the Bible and in the form of rational arguments. We will begin this study with a discussion of how to construct a logical argument, then define the claims we seek to prove, and finally show how to determine what evidence demonstrates the truth of these claims.

THE IMPORTANCE OF PROVIDING EVIDENCE

As we learned in Chapter 2, when we set out to investigate and verify the truth of Bahá'u'lláh, our approach must be in accordance with sound reasoning (*Paris Talks* 144), and this should characterize our investigation of religious claims about God and His Manifestations (*Promulgation* 227). As 'Abdu'l-Bahá says:

> reason must confirm it [religion] in order that it may inspire confidence. (*Promulgation* 394)

If an argument is to bear the test of reason, it must be based on solid evidence. This means that when we are speaking to

Christians our goal is to offer them reasonable arguments that
are based on, or convey, appropriate and sufficient biblical evidence to support the claims of the Bahá'í Faith. In this way,
our arguments will stand up to inquiry.

To apply this approach to our objective, we must present the evidence that justifies Bahá'u'lláh's claim to be a
Manifestation or Prophet of God. We must also show how this
evidence is consistent with the teachings of the Bible. But,
before we can set forth evidence, we must know what evidence is necessary and appropriate to prove Bahá'u'lláh's
claims. This requires that we understand what Bahá'u'lláh is
asserting when He claims to be a Manifestation or Prophet of
God.

DEFINITIONS OF THE TERMS 'MANIFESTATION' AND 'PROPHET'

When we say Bahá'u'lláh and Christ are 'Manifestations of
God,' or concisely, 'Manifestations,' we need to explain that
by this we mean: They manifest or reveal the attributes of
God. This is a simple and clear definition, provided there is
some understanding of what is intended by 'attributes of
God.' This phrase is common to both Christian commentaries
and books of doctrine and to the Bahá'í Faith. Therefore, this
is not generally a controversial point.

In the Bahá'í writings the terms 'Prophet' and 'Manifestation' are often equated, (e.g., *Kitáb-i-Íqán* 4, 6, 12–15, 80–1,
162–8, 178, 206, 219–20). 'Prophet' is frequently used in the
Bible and is applied with varying degrees of meaning. In a
narrow sense the term 'prophet' can be defined as simply one
who speaks prophetically. This appears to be Paul's meaning
when he ranks prophets below Apostles (1 Cor. 12:28). But
the term has also traditionally meant much more than simply
one who prophesies the future.

The term 'Prophet' is applied first in the Bible to Abraham
(Gen. 20:7), but Moses is considered by many Christians

to be the prototype of a Prophet of God.[41] In the Bible, Moses is the first to be described in a way which exemplifies all the characteristics that have come to be associated with the term 'Prophet.' Some of these characteristics are: the Prophet was called upon directly by God (Exod. 3), taught the knowledge of God (Exod. 3:15), legislated to the people (Deut. 24:19–22), sought to compel the people toward righteousness (Deut. 6:25), and possessed a prophetic awareness of history (Exod. 6). Such characteristics are generally typical of the biblical Prophets who came after Moses, such as Isaiah, Jeremiah and Zechariah.

However, another use of the term 'Prophet' is implied in the Bible. This is the "Messianic" type. Moses differs from all the prophets in the Old Testament who came after Him because He was the mediator of a new covenant. This covenant originated a new phase in Israel's religious life. All the prophets who came after Moses sought to propagate, establish, and maintain this new phase.

Jesus, however, was like Moses in that He was also an originator and mediator of a new covenant. Because Moses foretold "God will raise up for you a Prophet *like* me [Moses] from your midst" (Deut. 18:15, emphasis added), some Christian scholars have reasoned that this had to be a prophecy concerning the Messiah – meaning Jesus Christ. This is because, after Moses, only the Messiah (Jesus) was an originator and mediator of a new covenant (Heb. 8:6).[42] Christians find confirmation of this reasoning in Peter's quotation of this prophecy of Moses as support for the truth of Jesus (Acts 3:22).[43]

41. See *New Bible Dictionary* 980.

42. The prophecy of Moses, "God will raise up for you a Prophet like me" (Deut. 18:15) is commonly interpreted as referring to Christ. See, *Halley's Bible Handbook* 152; *The Interpretation of Prophecy* 178; *Matthew Henry's Commentary on the Whole Bible* (New 1 vol. edn.) 190; and *The New Bible Dictionary* 764–5.

43. The famous Bahá'í scholar Mírzá Abu'l-Faḍl argues that it is more likely that Deut. 18:18 refers to Muḥammad than Jesus. He bases this conclusion on a very literal reading of the term "brethren" (see Miracles and Metaphors 64). Mírzá Abu'l-Faḍl takes up this issue again noting that John 5:46 and

Christians believe Jesus to be in a category alone and above all other Prophets. Nevertheless, they recognize that Jesus is a Prophet like Moses, since both were the mediators of new covenants. This establishes a third definition of the term 'Prophet': the Messianic type. [44]

We have defined the term 'Prophet':

- In a limited sense, as those who only speak prophecies;
- In a general sense, as those who were called by God to guide Israel according to the laws and teachings established by Moses;
- And in the special sense, as those through whom God established a new covenant, the Messianic type.

Because Bahá'u'lláh established a new covenant, Bahá'ís believe Him to be a Prophet in the Messianic sense. To reiterate:

- When we say Bahá'u'lláh is a Manifestation, this means He manifests or reveals the attributes of God.
- When we say Bahá'u'lláh is a Prophet of God, this means He is a Prophet of the Messianic type, the mediator of a new covenant.

Acts 3:22–4 appear to contradict his view. He challenges the interpretation of John 5:46 and suggests that Luke's writings (the Book of Acts) are not infallible. He further states, apparently to bring Acts also into question, that "Luke was the disciple of Paul and had not himself attained the presence of Christ. His position is, therefore, equivalent to that of the second generation of early believers in the Islamic dispensation." (see *Mírzá Abu'l-Faḍl, Letters and Essays 1886–1913* 174–8.) In the opinion of this writer, Mírzá Abu'l-Faḍl is probably being too literal in his interpretation of the term "brethren." Although Deut. 18:18 is singular – "a prophet" – it is plausible that it can be equally applied to Jesus, Muḥammad and even the Báb and Bahá'u'lláh.

Also, Luke's testimony has support in that Paul knew Peter; Paul knew the Old Testament prophecies; and Luke very likely knew Peter also. It does not appear relevant whether Luke knew Christ, since Luke is quoting Peter from whom he may have heard a firsthand account of the events recorded in Acts. Also worth noting is that the Guardian lists Bible references to Muḥammad without mentioning Deut. 18:18 (*Lights of Guidance* 378).

44. 'Abdu'l-Bahá explains that two classes of Prophets exist, "One are the independent Prophets Who are followed; the other kind are not independent

Now that we have examined the nature of Bahá'u'lláh's claims, we must learn what type of evidence is necessary to support those claims.

THE PRINCIPLE THAT ALL THINGS ARE KNOWN BY THEIR QUALITIES

Chapter 4 discussed how everything in creation is identified by its own characteristic qualities and signs. This is the key principle we will use to identify the evidence that supports the truth of Bahá'u'lláh's claims. Bahá'u'lláh expresses this principle in these words:

> The proof of the sun is the light thereof, which shineth and envelopeth all things. (*Kitáb-i-Íqán* 209)

The same principle is embodied in Christ's statement:

> You will know them by their fruits. Do men gather grapes from thornbushes or figs from thistles? (Matt. 7: 16–17)

In these words, Christ emphasizes that things are known by their qualities or "fruits" and states that those qualities must be consistent with the reality of what they identify. For example, there is no relationship between grapes and thornbushes, nor between figs and thistles. Grapes come from grapevines, and because grapes are a fruit of the vine they are, in that way, consistent with the reality of the grapevine.

and are themselves followers" (*Some Answered Questions* 164). 'Abdu'l-Bahá lists as examples of the first type: Abraham, Moses, Christ, Muḥammad, the Báb, and Bahá'u'lláh. As examples of the second type He lists Solomon, David, Isaiah, Jeremiah, and Ezekiel (*Some Answered Questions*, ch. 43). Commonly, Christians speak of minor and major Prophets. These terms are generally intended to mean the authors of the prophetical Books, Isaiah through Malachi. The major Prophets are simply the Prophets the longer books are attributed to, who are: Isaiah, Jeremiah, Ezekiel, and Daniel. The rest are the minor Prophets. See *Halley's Bible Handbook* 280.

In the same way, divine perfections, that is, the attributes of God, are the qualities that characterize a Manifestation of God. When someone claims to be a Prophet, or Manifestation of God, we must therefore ask: Is the claimant characterized by the divine perfections we attribute to God?

This simple principle is true of all things, that is, all things are correctly recognized by their qualities (*Promulgation* 421–2). This is the principle Bahá'u'lláh is applying when He states that a Manifestation is known by His teachings (105–6, *Kitáb-i-Íqán* 205–6). The next chapter uses this approach to show exactly how Bahá'u'lláh's life and teachings indicate that He is a Manifestation of God.

1 0

IDENTIFYING AND
EXAMINING THE EVIDENCE

The last chapter determined what constitutes appropriate evidence for proving that Bahá'u'lláh is a Manifestation of God. Now we will study how to identify specific examples of such evidence and why it supports Bahá'u'lláh claims. We will also study how to support this approach with the Bible.

IDENTIFYING THE EVIDENCE

All things are known by the qualities that are appropriate to their realities. To study the qualities of a person's life, we can examine two broad categories: actions and words, or, in the case of a Prophet, His life – those things that He does – and His teachings – those things He says or writes. Thus, we will examine Bahá'u'lláh's life and teachings to find the qualities we will use as evidence to determine the truth of His claims.

This approach is suggested by Bahá'u'lláh, when He defined what constitutes the evidence, or testimony, that establishes the truth of a Manifestation:

The first and foremost testimony establishing His truth is His own Self. Next to this testimony is His Revelation. For whoso faileth to recognize either the one or the other He hath established the words He hath revealed as proof

of His reality and truth. This is, verily, an evidence of His
tender mercy unto men. He hath endowed every soul with
the capacity to recognize the signs of God. (*Gleanings*
105–6)

Since Bahá'u'lláh's earthly life ended with His passing in
1892, neither of the two foremost testimonies remain: we can
neither see Bahá'u'lláh, "His own self," nor can we hear His
revelation from Him personally. Consequently, we must learn
about both from what has been recorded. Therefore, "the
words He hath revealed," – His teachings – are His primary
testimony in the world today. Referring to verses of Scripture,
Bahá'u'lláh writes:

no testimony mightier than the testimony of their [the
Prophets'] revealed verses hath ever appeared upon the
earth. (*Kitáb-i-Íqán* 206)

To use the Scriptures as evidence, we must clearly understand
how they constitute the specific type of evidence necessary to
support the claims of Bahá'u'lláh. Claims to be a
Manifestation of God can only be warranted if the person's life
and teachings manifest divine qualities that are attributable to
God. Divine qualities are evidence of divinity. The same
evidence also allows us to determine what is the Word of
God, since we can define the Word of God as that which
reveals the divinity of God, or as that which is a revelation of
God.

We must keep in mind, though, that the words themselves
do not constitute evidence but, rather, the spiritual meaning
and intent conveyed through them. Therefore, when we say
that the words are the greatest evidence, we are really referring
to the meanings contained in the words. Furthermore, the
words of Scripture convey these teachings both by recording
the words revealed by the Manifestations and by recounting
their lives. Their lives impart teachings by way of example, and
we learn of their lives through written accounts.

So when we say the words of Scripture are evidence, the term *words* can be used to indicate *both* the Manifestations' *teachings* and the examples of their *lives*. It is equally true to say that the evidence of the Manifestations' truth is their teachings and their lives, or the Scriptures, which record both. Since we cannot directly witness Bahá'u'lláh living and teaching, we must turn to the records of His life and teachings, that is, the Bahá'í Scriptures. These writings are our primary source of evidence for determining that Bahá'u'lláh is a Manifestation of God.

AVOIDING CIRCULAR REASONING

When we speak of the word as proof of a Prophet's truth, we must be careful to avoid a common mistake. That mistake is usually referred to as circular reasoning. Circular reasoning is a fallacy committed when the conclusion to an argument is offered as the evidence, or premise, supporting the argument. For example, if you say the Bible is the Word of God because the Bible says it is the Word of God, this is a fallacy. The premise "the Bible *says* it is the word of God" has been used to support the conclusion that "the Bible *is* the word of God." Both premise and conclusion may be true, but the premise is not logically relevant to the purpose of proving the conclusion, and does not constitute adequate evidence for it.

Therefore, when we say the words of the Prophets are their greatest proof, it is *not* because the Prophets say the words are their greatest testimony. It is because the words reveal the divine attributes that indicate the words are from God, or because the words, at least, reflect that which we attribute to God. This spirituality is the evidence that justifies, and is the basis of, the claim. How Bahá'u'lláh's words reveal the divine attributes of God will be examined more closely in chapter 11.

EXAMINING THE EVIDENCE

When we consider the lives of the Prophets, we must go beyond the mere listing of the various events in their lives. We need to know *how* these actions and teachings reveal the attributes of God. Bahá'u'lláh points out in the *Kitáb-i-Íqán* that the suffering of the Manifestations, the act of sacrifice, reveals their significance:

> Examine the wondrous behavior of the Prophets, and recall the defamations and denials uttered by the children of negation and falsehood, perchance you may cause the bird of the human heart to wing its flight away from the abodes of heedlessness and doubt unto the nest of faith and certainty.... Should you acquaint yourself with the indignities heaped upon the Prophets of God, and apprehend the true causes of the objections voiced by their oppressors, you will surely appreciate the significance of their position. (*Kitáb-i-Íqán* 5–6)

When we consider how the Manifestations of God endure so many hardships, relinquishing the comforts of this world and becoming the objects of scorn and persecution, we see in their lives testimony of such divine qualities as purity, detachment, submission to the will of God, and unconditional love for humankind. It becomes clear and evident that their motives are to bring humanity to the divine Presence. Bahá'u'lláh gives us an example of this truth in His exposition on the proofs of the Báb:

> Another proof and evidence of the truth of this [the Báb's] Revelation, which amongst all other proofs shineth as the sun, is the constancy of the eternal Beauty in proclaiming the Faith of God. Though young and tender of age, and though the Cause He revealed was contrary to the desire of all the peoples of earth, both high and low, rich and poor, exalted and abased, king and subject, yet

He arose and steadfastly proclaimed it. All have known and heard this. He was afraid of no one; He was regardless of consequences. Could such a thing be made manifest except through the power of a divine Revelation, and the potency of God's invincible Will? (*Kitáb-i-Íqán* 230)

The Báb's quality of steadfastness during opposition testifies to the purity of His motives and that His purpose in enduring these trials was to bring us to God. Similarly, Peter writes:

For Christ also suffered once for sins, the just for the unjust, that He might bring us to God. (1 Pet. 3:18)

In the writings of Bahá'u'lláh we repeatedly find the same motive mentioned:

We, verily, have come for your sakes, and have borne the misfortunes of the world for your salvation. *(Tablets of Bahá'u'lláh* 10)

and:

My body hath endured imprisonment that ye may be released from the bondage of self. *(Tablets of Bahá'u'lláh* 12)

The Manifestations of God suffer for our sakes so as to free us from "the bondage of self" and to "bring us to God." In their willingness to suffer, we are able to perceive their divinity, because the persecution They endure for us reveals their attributes of love, forgiveness, and sovereignty. Hence, it can be argued that this is why They willingly suffer: to become a revelation of the attributes of God for humankind.

Their suffering stands as testimony to their patience, renunciation, self-sacrifice, transcendence, invincibility, and courage in the face of fierce opposition; their forgiveness, compassion, and love; and their trust in the providence of God. Their examples reveal those qualities that are divine, eternal, and fundamental to human happiness. In this way They reveal to humankind the spiritual life that we were all created to attain.

Such testimony is one of the most evident features in the accounts of the lives of the Prophets and explains why such emphasis is given in the sacred Books to this theme. The following examples examine how the suffering of the Manifestations reveals specific attributes of God.

How the Prophets manifest God's love

The specific attribute of love is revealed in the sacrifices the Manifestations of God have made for humankind. Christ says:

> Greater love has no one than this, than to lay down one's life for his friends. (John 15:13)

Christ, the Báb, Bahá'u'lláh and the other Prophets, however, offered their lives for all humankind, both friends and foe, a sacrifice which represents as great an evidence of love as we can ever conceive of. John writes:

> In this is love, not that we loved God, but that He loved us and sent His Son to be the propitiation for our sins. (1 John 4:10)

Similarly, Bahá'u'lláh writes:

> Fix your gaze upon Him Who is the Temple of God amongst men. He, in truth, hath offered up His life as a ransom for the redemption of the world. He, verily, is the All-Bountiful, the Gracious, the Most High. (*Gleanings* 315)

Since we are unable to conceive of a greater degree of love

than the Prophet's love of humanity, we naturally attribute it to divinity. 'Abdu'l-Bahá explains:

> What an infinite degree of love is reflected by the divine Manifestations toward mankind! For the sake of guiding the people They have willingly forfeited Their lives to resuscitate human hearts. They have accepted the cross. To enable human souls to attain the supreme degree of advancement, They have suffered during Their limited years extreme ordeals and difficulties. If Jesus Christ had not possessed love for the world of humanity, surely He would not have welcomed the cross. He was crucified for the love of mankind. Consider the infinite degree of that love. Without love for humanity John the Baptist would not have offered his life. It has been likewise with all the Prophets and Holy Souls. If the Báb had not manifested love for mankind, surely He would not have offered His breast for a thousand bullets. If Bahá'u'lláh had not been aflame with love for humanity, He would not have willingly accepted forty years' imprisonment. (*Promulgation* 256–7)

How the Prophets manifest God's power and sovereignty

It is an axiom that God is all powerful, and His sovereignty endures for all time. Likewise, there is no greater evidence of power and sovereignty existing in the world than that which the Manifestations of God exercise over the hearts and consciences of humanity. It is pervasive and enduring.

Their followers, so transformed by the Manifestations' influence, have decided time and again to renounce their possessions, even their lives, rather than recant their beliefs. Diverse groups with the most violent antagonisms have been united in common agreement. Social harmony has prevailed over strife, and the resulting cooperation has given rise to new civilizations.

The influence of the Manifestations survives the passage of centuries. No ruler, scientist, philosopher, poet or artist has ever had such an enduring and pervasive influence on humankind. It is only to the Manifestations that people still faithfully turn even after hundreds of years have passed. No one in history has ever equaled the Manifestations of God in their sovereignty.[45]

Forgiveness and the other attributes of God

The further we contemplate the lives of the Manifestations the more we will be able to perceive the evidences of their divine virtues and qualities. The greatest measure of forgiveness is apparent in the way They forgave not only their loved ones but also their oppressors, and even extended their forgiveness to any repentant man or woman, no matter how villainous.

Their lives testify to their innate knowledge, graciousness, majesty, forbearance, mercy, fearlessness, and many other spiritual perfections. The unbiased observer who becomes acquainted with and who reflects on the lives of the Prophets will readily acknowledge that They are the greatest examples of perfection evident to the world.

A DISTINCTION BETWEEN GREAT PEOPLE AND PROPHETS

Some may argue that many people suffer, and some even sacrifice their lives for noble causes, but this does not make them Prophets of God. This observation is correct. Prophets are not the only examples of such virtues in the world. However, our purpose is to demonstrate that They are the greatest examples of such virtues and the most perfect in every way,

---

45. Bahá'u'lláh discusses in detail the sovereignty of the Manifestations in the *Kitáb-i-Íqán* (106–34).

and that their perfections became evident both because They suffered and due to the reason for their suffering.

God is, to humankind, the ultimate embodiment of love, justice, forgiveness, and all other divine perfections. It is because Christ, Bahá'u'lláh, and other Prophets possess such perfections that we say They manifest what we attribute to God. Hence, we refer to Them as Manifestations of the attributes of God, or simply, Manifestations. Therefore, whoever among humankind, such as Christ, Buddha and Bahá'u'lláh, shows the *greatest* degree of these perfections and puts forth the claim, we appropriately designate a Manifestation of God.

THE LIMITATION OF HUMAN PERCEPTION

When contemplating the attributes of God and the lives of the Manifestations, we must keep in mind the limitations of our own human perception. For example, we believe that God is all-knowing and accept that Christ and Bahá'u'lláh reflect this divine attribute. We can contemplate and demonstrate to some measure that their spiritual knowledge is extremely profound and far reaching – in fact, we are compelled to say, immeasurable. And therein lies our problem. Being immeasurable, it is beyond our ability to prove its extent; whether it has a limit or is limitless. To give a simplistic example: It is not possible to ask the Prophets all the possible spiritual questions and discover whether any limits to their knowledge exist. One can only say that, in Them, the greatest examples of spiritual knowledge are perceived (see *Promulgation* 113–14).

THE BIBLICAL BASIS FOR THE BAHÁ'Í CONCEPT OF EVIDENCE

Even though the Bible does not explicitly state that the verses or words of Scripture are the primary proof of a Prophet, it states this truth indirectly. This can be demonstrated because the Bible indicates that the ability of a Prophet to impart the Word of God is essential to His ability to give us salvation and eternal life. This makes the Word of God a clear biblical criterion for determining a true Manifestation of God.

For example, Paul tells us that we are "saved through faith" (Eph. 2:8) but that "faith comes by hearing, and hearing by the word of God" (Rom. 10:17).[46] Christ states:

> Most assuredly, I say to you, he who hears My word and believes in Him who sent Me has everlasting life, and shall not come into judgment but has passed from death to life. (John 5:24)

Furthermore, Christ states that we must be "born again" (John 3:3), and Peter writes that we are born again "through the word of God." (1 Pet. 1:23)

Since we gain faith (Rom. 10:17), rebirth (1 Pet. 1:23), and everlasting life (John 5:24) through the Word of God, the ability to mediate the Word of God must be the primary quality of a true Manifestation of God.

For example, if we are saved by the Word of God, then for Jesus to be our Saviour He must be able to impart the Word of God. If Jesus did impart the word of God, He would have given us that which, according to the Bible, is essential for our salvation. He would be our saviour. The evidence that He is Saviour is the fact that He imparted the Word of God, whereby souls were saved.

All of these points show how the Word of God, which is expressed through the life and teachings of Christ, is the primary means by which Christ accomplished His purpose to "save His people from their sins" (Matt. 1:21) and to bring us into "everlasting life" (John 3:16). Therefore, the ability to

46. Since the Scriptures say we are "saved through faith" (Eph. 2:8), some may argue that it is not the Word but faith that saves. However, Paul makes the important link when he points out "faith comes by hearing, and hearing by the word of God" (Rom. 10:17). The faith that saves ultimately rests upon the Word of God.

impart the Word of God is a primary and essential characteristic, or quality, of Christ. This also suggests the preeminent nature of the Word of God and its inseparability from Christ or from anyone who is truly a Manifestation of God.[47]

Since we are saved through the Word of God, then from the point of view of our salvation, anyone who claims to be a Manifestation of God must be characterized by the ability to impart the Word of God. If we hear Bahá'u'lláh's words and perceive that they are, in fact, the words of God, then they stand as evidence in support of Bahá'u'lláh's claim.

This suggests the true meaning of salvation. A Manifestation of God reveals divine qualities through His example and teachings. These divine qualities influence our lives, and this change brings about our salvation. These points supply a biblical explanation as to why Bahá'u'lláh offers the "words He hath revealed as proof of His reality and truth" (*Gleanings* 105). We will now consider how best to present the evidence we have just learned.

47. This understanding of the relationship between the Word of God and the Manifestations suggests the significance and meaning of "the Word became flesh and dwelt among us" (John 1:14).

11

PRESENTING
THE EVIDENCE

We have examined how the lives and suffering of the Manifestations reveal their divine attributes. Now we need to learn how we can present this evidence to Christians. One way to improve our presentation skills is to study how Paul presented the message of Christ and how 'Abdu'l-Bahá presented the message of Bahá'u'lláh.

HOW SAINT PAUL MADE KNOWN THE DIVINE QUALITIES OF CHRIST

Paul, the chief propagator of Christianity after Christ, greatly emphasizes the significance of the suffering Christ bore for humankind. Rather than recount the miracles of Christ or mention such events as the virgin birth, Paul speaks of Christ's sacrifice. Paul's approach is probably best summarized in these words:

> For Jews request a sign, and Greeks seek after wisdom; but we preach Christ crucified, to the Jews a stumbling block and to the Greeks foolishness, but to those who are called, both Jews and Greeks, Christ the power of God and the wisdom of God. (1 Cor. 1:22–24)

The Jews thought the power of God was to be seen in miracles, but Paul knew the pure in heart would see the power of God revealed in Jesus' triumph despite His crucifixion. The Greeks sought wisdom through the philosophies of men, but Paul knew the pure in heart would see in the suffering of Jesus a greater wisdom, a wisdom that leads to the knowledge of spiritual realities, a knowledge of God. Therefore, Paul preached "the message of the cross" (1 Cor. 1:18). This message pointed out the qualities of divine power and spiritual wisdom revealed through Jesus' sacrifice. For the same reason, 'Abdu'l-Bahá emphasized the suffering of Bahá'u'lláh.

HOW 'ABDU'L-BAHÁ MADE KNOWN THE DIVINE QUALITIES OF BAHÁ'U'LLÁH

On numerous occasions 'Abdu'l-Bahá wrote and spoke about Bahá'u'lláh's life, and in each account the sacrifice of Bahá'u'lláh was an essential theme. 'Abdu'l-Bahá makes the following points when referring to the suffering of Bahá'u'lláh:

> If Bahá'u'lláh had not been aflame with love for humanity, He would not have willingly accepted forty years' imprisonment. (*Promulgation* 257)

> There was no ordeal or difficulty He [Bahá'u'lláh] did not experience, yet He endured all in perfect joy and happiness. (*Promulgation* 383)

> Bahá'u'lláh endured forty years of vicissitudes, ordeals and hardships for the purpose of spreading His teachings. (*Promulgation* 372)

> His [Bahá'u'lláh's] life was a vortex of persecution and difficulty; yet catastrophes, extreme ordeals and vicissitudes did not hinder the accomplishment of His work and

mission. Nay, on the contrary, His power became greater and greater. (*Promulgation* 145)

He bore these ordeals, suffered these calamities and difficulties in order that a manifestation of selflessness and service might become apparent in the world of humanity; that the Most Great Peace should become a reality. (*Promulgation* 28)

In these passages, 'Abdu'l-Bahá shows how Bahá'u'lláh manifested the "fruit of the Spirit" (Gal. 5:22) – love, joy, peace, and long-suffering – even though He was persecuted. By pointing out Bahá'u'lláh's happiness, 'Abdu'l-Bahá shows that true spiritual happiness is not dependent on the comforts of this world and that through living a spiritual life we too can attain happiness despite the difficulties we encounter.

'Abdu'l-Bahá states that Bahá'u'lláh suffered these ordeals to spread His teachings. Through His suffering, "love and unity were established, and the differing religions found a center of contact and reconciliation" (*Promulgation* 145–6). 'Abdu'l-Bahá states:

Therefore, we also must strive in this pathway of love and service, sacrificing life and possessions, passing our days in devotion, consecrating our efforts wholly to the Cause of God so that, God willing, the ensign of universal religion may be uplifted in the world of mankind and the oneness of the world of humanity be established. (*Promulgation* 146)

In this passage, 'Abdu'l-Bahá points out that the love of humanity, apparent in Bahá'u'lláh's willingness to suffer exiles and imprisonments for us, exerts a powerful influence on our hearts. It motivates and inspires us to change, and to transform the hostilities of the world into peace and unity. 'Abdu'l-Bahá also assures us of the ultimate triumph of good by repeatedly reminding us that none of these hardships ever hindered Bahá'u'lláh from accomplishing His mission.

These points from 'Abdu'l-Bahá's talks illustrate why so much emphasis is placed on Bahá'u'lláh's exiles and imprisonments. Today the "message of the cross" is the message of Bahá'u'lláh's imprisonments. Bahá'u'lláh clearly and eloquently states the meaning of this message in these verses:

> My body hath endured imprisonment that ye may be released from the bondage of self. (*Tablets of Bahá'u'lláh* 12)

> We, verily, have come for your sakes, and have borne the misfortunes of the world for your salvation. (*Tablets of Bahá'u'lláh* 10)

We have examined how 'Abdu'l-Bahá used the example of Bahá'u'lláh's life to reveal the divine qualities that support His claim to be a Manifestation of God. Now, we will consider how 'Abdu'l-Bahá presented the words, or teachings, of Bahá'u'lláh to demonstrate the truth of this claim.

Since Bahá'u'lláh's teachings are "boundless and illimitable" (*Promulgation* 457), we must first decide which ones to present in our discussions. If we study *The Promulgation of Universal Peace*, we see that 'Abdu'l-Bahá repeatedly mentions Bahá'u'lláh's teachings on the independent investigation of truth, the oneness of humanity, the equality of men and women, the unity of religion, the harmony of science and religion, the promotion of a world government, and world peace – all principles that are regarded as central teachings of Bahá'u'lláh's Faith.

'Abdu'l-Bahá points out that such teachings constitute a means for reconciling conflict in all spheres of human life and for fostering love and unity among all peoples. He calls our attention to the essential spiritual, self-evident truths underlying these teachings, truths that are inherent in – and thus common to – all divinely revealed religions. As an example, let's examine 'Abdu'l-Bahá's presentation of Bahá'u'lláh's teaching about the oneness of humankind:

> First [of these principles], that the oneness of humanity shall be recognized and established. All men are the servants of God. He has created all; He is the Provider and Preserver; He is loving to all. Inasmuch as He is just and kind, why should we be unjust toward each other? ... Therefore, we must follow the will and plan of God. As He is kind to all, we must be likewise; and it is certain that this will be most acceptable to God. (*Promulgation* 127)

'Abdu'l-Bahá explains that we should love all people because God loves all people. He urges His audience to accept Bahá'u'lláh's teaching of the oneness of humankind because it is a teaching that reflects the loving nature of God. In this way, 'Abdu'l-Bahá draws the audience's attention to the divine nature of Bahá'u'lláh's teachings: how they manifest the all-loving quality of God. Furthermore, this teaching, when practiced, fosters the love that it embodies and is therefore evidence we can directly perceive. We can, ourselves, experience its truth when interacting with people of diverse national, racial, and cultural backgrounds.

An example illustrating the divine attributes of fairness and justice inherent in Bahá'u'lláh's teachings can be seen in 'Abdu'l-Bahá's discussion of the equality of men and women:

> The one whose heart is most pure, whose deeds and service in the Cause of God are greater and nobler, is most acceptable before the divine threshold – whether male or female....Why should man, who is endowed with the sense of justice and sensibilities of conscience, be willing that one of the members of the human family should be rated and considered as subordinate? Such differentiation is neither intelligent nor conscientious; therefore, the principle of religion has been revealed by Bahá'u'lláh that woman must be given the privilege of

equal education with man and full right to his preroga-
tives. That is to say, there must be no difference in the
education of male and female in order that womankind
may develop equal capacity and importance with man in
the social and economic equation. (*Promulgation* 108)

Through such explanations, 'Abdu'l-Bahá brings to our conscious awareness the divine nature of Bahá'u'lláh's teachings.
Since Bahá'u'lláh's teachings manifest the qualities of God,
we find in them evidence that Bahá'u'lláh is a Manifestation of
God. Because these teachings are so broad in their reach, it is
impossible to conceive of teachings more perfect or more
capable of expressing God's love in the world today. Bahá-
'u'lláh's teachings are not just for the benefit of one race or
nation, but rather, the whole world. So essential is it for
religious teachings to reflect the attributes of God that
'Abdu'l-Bahá advises the abandonment of any religion that
contradicts this divine imperative:

> Among the teachings of Bahá'u'lláh is His declaration
> that religion must be the cause of love and fellowship,
> must be the source of unity in the hearts of men. If relig-
> ion becomes a cause of enmity and hatred, it is evident
> that the abolition of religion is preferable to its promulga-
> tion; for religion is a remedy for human ills. If a remedy
> should be productive of disease, it is certainly advisable to
> abandon it. (*Promulgation* 373)

There are many different ways in which 'Abdu'l-Bahá sums up
Bahá'u'lláh's central teachings. However, the important point
is the way 'Abdu'l-Bahá stresses their underlying divine
character. The following example illustrates this approach:

> The essential principles of His healing remedies are the
> knowledge and love of God, severance from all else save
> God, turning our faces in sincerity toward the King-
> dom of God, implicit faith, firmness and fidelity, loving-

kindness toward all creatures and the acquisition of the divine virtues indicated for the human world. These are the fundamental principles of progress, civilization, international peace and the unity of mankind. These are the essentials of Bahá'u'lláh's teachings, the secret of everlasting health, the remedy and healing for man. (*Promulgation* 205)

One way to verify the truth of this statement is simply to experience that healing in our own lives. The patient who takes the doctor's advice and who personally finds it to be an effective remedy can best testify to that doctor's credentials.

THE IMPORTANCE OF OUR PERSONAL EXPERIENCE WHEN PRESENTING THE PROOFS OF BAHÁ'U'LLÁH

The experience we have as believers is a very important source of evidence to use when we present Bahá'í proofs. For example, 'Abdu'l-Bahá repeatedly challenges those who question the practicability of Bahá'u'lláh's teachings and calls attention to the fact that their effect and workability is already evident in the experience of the believers:

Antagonism and strife have passed away; love and agreement have taken the place of hatred and animosity. Furthermore, those souls who have followed Bahá'u'lláh and attained this condition of fellowship and affiliation are Muslims, Jews, Christians, Zoroastrians, Buddhists, Nestorians, Sunnites, Shiites and others. No discord exists among them. This is a proof of the possibility of unification among the religionists of the world through practical means. (*Promulgation* 234)

The practice of Bahá'u'lláh's teachings in our personal lives gives us a direct means of experiencing and knowing the truth of their divinity. 'Abdu'l-Bahá states:

The proof of the validity of a Manifestation of God is the penetration and potency of His Word, the cultivation of heavenly attributes in the hearts and lives of His followers and the bestowal of divine education upon the world of humanity. This is absolute proof. The world is a school in which there must be Teachers of the Word of God. The evidence of the ability of these Teachers is efficient education of the graduating classes. (*Promulgation* 341)

The truth that proof of the divinity of the teachings can be known directly through practicing them is also expressed in these words of Christ:

My doctrine is not Mine, but His who sent Me. If anyone wants to do His will, he shall know concerning the doctrine, *whether* it is from God or whether I speak on My own *authority*. (John 7:17)

The way to experience this evidence personally is by allowing the qualities of the Manifestation, that is, the divine perfections of His life and teachings, to influence our own lives.

We can acquire knowledge either indirectly or directly. For example, if we want to know the truth of the existence of the ocean, we can either inquire about the matter by asking others, or we can seek to acquire knowledge directly by going to the ocean and experiencing it for ourselves. Even though the limitations of our perception do not allow us to perceive all of the ocean at once, directly experiencing it for ourselves still remains the most certain means of verification.

People often believe many things without knowing if these things are actually true. Experience helps us attain the knowledge to confirm our beliefs. To state this another way, we can personally turn to the Scriptures for evidence, and we can personally experience that evidence by allowing its message to influence our lives and by practicing the prescribed teachings.

The degree to which we can directly know the evidence of Bahá'u'lláh depends on the degree to which we allow the message of Bahá'u'lláh to influence our lives. This type of evidence is not uniquely confined to the Bahá'í Faith. The sincere followers of other religions can also know the divine realities of their Faiths by the spiritual influence on their lives. Furthermore, Christians who have had a positive religious experience will naturally resist the Bahá'í Faith if they mistakenly think this will lead to abandoning their own faith.

Some Christians speak of what they popularly refer to as "a personal relationship with Christ." This relationship usually involves the experience of how their belief in Christ has changed their lives. Frequently, such a personal relationship also includes a type of communication with Christ. Typically this communication consists of talking to Jesus through prayer and perceiving a response from Jesus in the events that transpire, which are believed to be related to these prayers. Many Christians place great importance on having this type of relationship.

When Christians seek to convert others to their Faith, they often talk about their own experiences as a way of giving evidence for the truth of Christ. This type of presentation tends to be comprised of a simple description of how their lives have changed for the better since they became a believer in Christ. Sharing this type of evidence with non-believers is sometimes referred to as "giving a personal testimonial" or "witnessing."

This type of presentation is compelling to receptive people because it offers them the promise of a better life. Moreover, it is evidence they can put to the test by accepting Christ for themselves and following His teachings.

People may see little reason to accept Bahá'u'lláh if they are unable to see how Bahá'u'lláh can change their lives in a positive way or can help the world. Therefore, when we talk with Christians we should consider, and be prepared to explain, how Bahá'u'lláh is, in fact, transforming people's lives and how His message will benefit the world.

We can be better prepared to give this type of testimony if we first consciously reflect on what our own lives would be like had we not discovered the Bahá'í Faith. We should consider the spiritual changes that have occurred in our lives since we accepted Bahá'u'lláh. For example, we can think about how our personal experiences with Bahá'u'lláh have brought us closer to God, have provided us with guidance, and have given us the strength, courage, and inner peace to rise to the challenges of life's tests and misfortunes. Being a Bahá'í takes away our despair at our shortcomings and past errors and gives us hope even amid all the world's problems.

We should also consider what the message of Bahá'u'lláh has accomplished for others. It is not difficult to see how Bahá'u'lláh has made many people become concerned and loving toward others about whom they might otherwise not have cared. For example, Bahá'ís are clearly known for their sensitivity to and concern with the injustices people of other races are suffering.

By being aware of how Bahá'u'lláh has influenced our lives and the lives of others, we will be better able to explain why we are Bahá'ís and to help Christians understand Bahá'u'lláh's spiritual power and truth. As Peter says:

> always *be* ready to *give* a defense to everyone who asks you a reason for the hope that is in you. (1 Pet. 3:15)

The next chapter will consider some of the questions and problems involving prophesies, miracles, and doctrines that we are likely to encounter when presenting proofs of Bahá'u-'lláh's claims.

12

SOME PROBLEMS
AND QUESTIONS

BEING PREPARED FOR POSSIBLE OBSTACLES

Before we are able to conclude a presentation of proofs establishing the truth of Bahá'u'lláh, we may encounter objections related to popular Christian beliefs. For example, many Christians believe the proof of Christianity is expressed in the doctrine of the physical resurrection of Jesus Christ; thus they may reject Bahá'u'lláh's claim on the grounds that, unlike Christ, He did not triumph over physical death. Furthermore, some Christians may object to the Bahá'í argument on the grounds that it contradicts the doctrine of atonement and the doctrine of original sin, as well as the belief that Jesus is superior to all other Prophets and is exclusively perfect.

In many cases it may be necessary to enter a discussion about such doctrines with the hope of later returning to our original presentation. When we attempt to answer such doctrinal questions, we should present our answers in such a way as to show that while the interpretations involved in some Christian doctrines appear to contradict the Bahá'í view, the actual text of the Bible does not necessarily suggest such contradictions.

We should also keep in mind that it is possible to become completely sidetracked when answering questions related to Christian doctrines. Our task is not to debate doctrines, as

Christians have themselves done for centuries. Rather, we should stay focused on presenting the proofs of Bahá'u'lláh. To avoid the problem of becoming sidetracked, it is important that we present our overall argument simply and concisely at the beginning. Then when we attempt to answer additional and related questions we can discuss them in a way that supports our original theme. If the Christian is aware of the basic points of our presentation, he or she will be able to perceive, as each doctrine is discussed, how those points can remain acceptable in the broader scheme of the Bible and how they relate to our original argument. Otherwise, we risk losing our opportunity to present the proofs of Bahá'u'-lláh.

Another difficulty we may encounter concerns criteria. If we are not careful, this issue can trap us in an interminable disagreement. Stated simply: Bahá'ís believe that the teachings of Bahá'u'lláh are the criteria establishing His truth (*Promulgation* 364). Christians feel they cannot accept that Bahá'u'lláh's teachings are from God because His teachings do not agree with the Christian interpretation of the Bible. Bahá'ís believe the Bible is in agreement with Bahá'u'lláh and His teachings and that disagreements or conflicts exist because of human interpretations – not because of an actual conflict with the Bible. At the heart of this conflict is the disagreement over what the Bible truly teaches.

Such conflicts leave no alternative except to present both views and let the listener make his or her own choice. There is no sure way to present the proofs of Bahá'u'lláh so that every listener will perceive the spiritual perfections embodied in those teachings. But remember, our responsibility does not involve making decisions of faith for others. Our task is to do the best we can to demonstrate that such criteria are a reliable basis for faith.

Knowledge and familiarity with the basic principles of our arguments will help us consciously overcome the obstacles of human opinions, speculations, and mistaken interpretations. It is to be hoped that will help us convey to Christians that

spiritual attributes not complex doctrines form a reliable basis
for decisions of faith.

QUESTIONS AND ANSWERS

Answers to a few questions concerning prophecies, miracles,
and doctrines are presented in the remaining pages of this
chapter. When discussing the proofs of Bahá'u'lláh, all of
these types of questions are very likely to arise. A more thorough examination of Christian doctrines may be found in
Volume Two, while Volume Three presents a more exhaustive
study of Christian prophecy. It should be borne in mind that
the questions considered in this chapter are simplifications of
more involved issues, and their answers likewise are designed
to be brief. The answers given here represent only one way of
addressing these questions and are intended to serve as partial
examples of how to introduce a broader discussion of the
issues.

Questions concerning prophecies

Question: Does the Old Testament teach that the true test
of a Prophet is that His prophecies come true?
Have the prophecies of Bahá'u'lláh come true?
And if prophecy is the true test of a prophet, are
we not deviating from the correct criteria by investigating His life and teachings instead of first
checking to see if Bahá'u'lláh's prophecies came
true?

Answer: The prophecies of Bahá'u'lláh have in many cases
already come true and are mentioned, for ex-
ample, by Shoghi Effendi in such books as *The
Promised Day Is Come* and *The World Order of
Bahá'u'lláh*. Concerning prophecy as a criteria,

the Old Testament states that if a Prophet's words do not come to pass, he is a false prophet. However, if the words do come to pass he may still be a false prophet.[48] If someone says something will happen and it does happen, how do you know the event occurred *because* they said it would? This means that we cannot judge Bahá'u'lláh's prophecies on the basis of their fulfillment. Only in the case of unfulfilled prophecies is such a presumption justified. The text reads, "if the thing does not happen or come to pass, that is the thing which the Lord has not spoken; *the prophet* has spoken it presumptuously; you shall not be afraid of him" (Deut. 18:22, emphasis added).

Question: Rather than examining Bahá'u'lláh's life and teachings, wouldn't it be better to simply ascertain whether or not He fulfilled biblical prophecy?

Answer: Bahá'u'lláh has, in fact, fulfilled biblical prophecy. But before we can see how His life relates to prophecy we must *first* examine and understand its spiritual significance. We should keep in mind that the Jews did not realize that Christ had fulfilled the prophecies because they did not percieve the real significance of His station. This problem is only one of the reasons why prophecy is not a very conclusive form of proof.

Many prophecies, as in the Book of Revelation, are written in a very symbolic manner. How can we be sure we are interpreting these complex and mysterious prophecies correctly in order to know whether or not they have in fact come true? Even among Christian scholars there are numerous debates concerning the meaning of such prophecies.

48. See *New Bible Dictionary* 980.

Some prophecies are impossible to verify. The virgin birth of Jesus is one such example. Even though we accept the reality of the virgin birth, which is the fulfillment of Isaiah 7:13–14 (see also Matt. 1:23), and which provides proof of Isaiah's prophethood, we nevertheless accept it solely on the testimony of the Scripture (the New Testament, the Qur'án and the Bahá'í writings), for otherwise it is impossible to verify. Therefore, if we accept the Prophethood of Isaiah, or even Jesus, on the basis of such a prophecy, and we accept its fulfillment as true solely on testimony and without any other evidence, then do we also accept other claims to prophethood even though we are only given testimony without verification? Proof without verifiable evidence presupposes acceptance and is, therefore, unconvincing.

Another difficulty is that many prophecies only constitute circumstantial evidence in that they pertain to events and circumstances around the Prophet, but do not actually indicate one Prophet to the exclusion of others who make the same claims. If a prophecy states an event will occur, but when it does many individuals claim to be the promised Prophet, how do you know which one is the true Prophet? This is why we must ultimately rely on the evidence of their divine perfections.

Questions concerning miracles

Question: Many miraculous events are associated with the Prophets of God in the Bible. The Gospels recorded that Jesus was born miraculously, performed many miracles in His ministry, and was then miraculously resurrected. Miracles characterize all the Prophets. Therefore, it seems that a true Prophet must perform miracles. Can Bahá'u'lláh prove His claims by miracles?

Answer: According to the Bahá'í teachings, all Prophets perform miracles (*Some Answered Questions* 100–2), and indeed a proof of Bahá'u'lláh is the "miracles He performed" (*Selections from the Writings of 'Abdu'l-Bahá* 16). However, Bahá'u'-'lláh counsels us not to recount miracles (*Epistle* 33). 'Abdu'l-Bahá explains:

> many wonderful things [miracles] were done by Bahá'u'lláh, but we do not recount them, as they do not constitute proofs and evidences for all the peoples of the earth, and they are not decisive proofs even for those who see them: they may think that they are merely enchantments. (*Some Answered Questions* 45)

Obviously, it is preferable to rest our faith on the most solid ground. 'Abdu'l-Bahá points out that it is not possible to consider events that none of us are able to witness personally as incontrovertible proof. We are unable to prove that the miracles recorded in the Holy Text are actual instances of the contravention of the laws of nature and not symbolic accounts written to convey spiritual truths. Furthermore, even if we accept these miracles as proof, how do we distinguish them from the miracles attributed to other persons?[49]

49. 'Abdu'l-Bahá cites the problem of discriminating between the claims of miracles asserted in different religious traditions (see *Some Answered Questions*, chs. 10 and 22).

There are at least two biblical passages indicating that miracles are not the "fruits" Christ advises us to stake our faith on:

1 Jesus indicates that we should not ask for, or seek, signs (i.e., miracles) when He stated: "An evil and adulterous generation seeks after a sign" (Matt. 12:39)

2 Jesus indicates that the working of miracles is not limited to true Prophets when He said: "For false christs and false prophets will arise and show great signs and wonders, so as to deceive, if possible, even the elect." (Matt. 24 :24)

If the Bible states we should not seek miracles and if we know that someone who works or claims to work miracles may well be a false prophet, how can we use miracles as a criterion for divinity? Once again, it is evident that we must ultimately rely on the evidence of their divine perfections.

Question: Does this mean Bahá'ís do not believe that miracles and prophecies constitute evidence for establishing the truth of a Prophet?

Answer: According to the Bahá'í point of view both prophecies and miracles constitute evidence of a true Prophet. However, such evidence is not regarded as conclusive. Problems, such as the verification of the performance of miracles and the fulfillment of prophecies, make miracles and prophecies too unreliable. However, the teachings of the Prophet can be heard by everyone. Since the teachings reflect the divine perfections of God, and everyone can hear or read the teachings for themselves, the teachings are the most verifiable and reliable testimony that the Prophet is a Manifestation of God. These reasons indicate why the teachings are the "greatest" proof.

Question: In the Book of Acts it is written:

> Men of Israel, hear these words: Jesus of Nazareth, a Man attested by God to you by miracles, wonders, and signs which God did through Him in your midst, as you yourselves also know. (Acts 2:22)

How can miracles be refuted as proof if Peter offers miracles as evidence?

Answer: Peter is speaking of miracles performed through Christ in their "midst." Because Peter's audience had seen these miracles, to them they constituted proof. The text does not suggest that one should rely exclusively on miracles. Also, we have assumed that the text means "miracles" in the literal and physical sense. It is worth noting that this is an interpretation of which we cannot be sure. Many of the miracles performed by Christ have been explained in a number of reasonable ways. The Bible itself sometimes suggests a symbolic meaning. For instance, in the Gospel according to Matthew it is recorded that Christ fed an entire multitude with only seven loaves of bread (Matt. 15). However, shortly after, Christ equates the leaven of bread with doctrines (Matt. 16:5–12). Therefore, the miracle of feeding the multitude can be understood as Jesus imparting the Word of God. The Bible equates Jesus with both the Word of God (John 1:1–14) and the "bread of God" (John 6:33). As long as there is a reasonable and spiritual explanation, there is no compelling reason to insist that the miracle involved intervention in the laws of nature. Moreover, since most miracles may be symbols concerning the teachings of God, Peter's reference to such spiritual miracles may be another way of referring to the teachings.

Questions concerning doctrines

Question: The suffering of Bahá'u'lláh has been mentioned as proof that He is a Manifestation of God. However, Christ suffered once for all time (Heb. 9:23–8), which seems to indicate that there is no need for another Manifestation of God. Also, Christians do not believe Christ will suffer again when He returns. Therefore, why does humankind need Bahá'u'lláh, and how can He be the return of Christ if He has suffered?

Answer: It is true that Christ offered Himself as a sacrifice once for all time. That sacrifice was also completely sufficient. According to Bahá'í belief, it is not the insufficiency of past Prophets that brings about the unfolding of a new Revelation, it is rather the incompetency and waywardness of humankind.[50] That Bahá'u'lláh suffered for

50. "In the Bayán the Báb says that every religion of the past was fit to become universal. The only reason why they failed to attain that mark was the incompetence of their followers. He then proceeds to give a definite promise that this would not be the fate of the revelation of 'Him Whom God would make manifest,' that it would become universal and include all the people of the world. This shows that we will ultimately succeed. But could we not through our shortcomings, failures to sacrifice and reluctance to concentrate our efforts in spreading the Cause, retard the realization of that ideal? And what would that mean? It shall mean that we will be held responsible before God, and that the race will remain longer in its state of wayward-

humanity is yet another sign of God's unfailing grace toward humankind. Concerning the renewal of religion 'Abdu'l-Bahá said:

> Now, consider: Christ frequently repeated that the Ten Commandments in the Pentateuch were to be followed, and He insisted that they should be maintained. Among the Ten Commandments is one which says: 'Do not worship any picture or image.' At present in some of the Christian churches many pictures and images exist. It is, therefore, clear and evident that the Religion of God does not maintain its original principles among the people, but that it has gradually changed and altered until it has been entirely destroyed and annihilated. Because of this the manifestation is renewed, and a new religion established. But if religions did not change and alter, there would be no need of renewal. (*Some Answered Questions* 165–6)

Concerning the return of Christ, the Bible testifies that Christ will come back to defeat the armies of darkness which will wage war against Him (Rev. 19:19–20). This prophecy states that Christ will be opposed but that He will prevail. Interpreted literally: Christ destroys His opponents militarily. But if we interpret these passages symbolically, they can be understood as foretelling that He will be persecuted, will again suffer, and through this sacrifice will be victorious over His enemies.

ness, that wars would not soon be averted, that human suffering will last longer." (From a letter dated February 20, 1932, written on behalf of Shoghi Effendi to the National Spiritual Assembly of the United States and Canada.)

Question: How can Bahá'u'lláh's suffering be equated with Christ's death on the cross. Bahá'u'lláh suffered, but Christ was actually crucified.

Answer: Both Christ and Bahá'u'lláh suffered for the same reason, "the remission of sins" (*Some Answered Questions* 125). The amount or type of ordeal is not the most significant factor. Rather, it is the reason for the suffering and the station or quality of the one who suffered that matters. This is the essential difference between the Prophets' suffering and the suffering experienced by other people. Both Christ and Bahá'u'lláh suffered, even though they were innocent, to transform the lives of people who are guilty of many sins. Their suffering can be equated because both the suffering of Bahá'u'lláh and of Christ cause the qualities of divinity to be revealed to us.[51]

Question: Even if Bahá'u'lláh manifests the attributes of God, why should anyone cease to follow Christ exclusively, since Christ remains perfect for all time?

Answer: It is true that Christ is perfect for all time. "Jesus Christ is the same yesterday, today, and forever" (Heb. 13:8). Turning to Bahá'u'lláh is not a turning away from Christ, but an acknowledgment of the fulfillment of Christ's promises and prophecies. There is never a turning away from Christ. If

---

51. This equation concerns the revelation of divine perfections but not the doctrine of atonement as traditionally believed by Christians. This distinction will become clear in the forthcoming volume of *Preparing for a Bahá'í/Christian Dialogue, Understanding Christian Beliefs* (Volume Two), which contains explanations concerning the doctrine of substitutionary atonement.

Christ has returned, it is recognizing that return which keeps one turned toward Christ. *This response is what the Bahá'í Faith is about.*

BIBLICAL REFERENCES

For easy reference to the biblical information used in the arguments presented in Part Three, we can make an outline of the following verses in our Bibles. To highlight the verses, use a green marker to signify the category "criteria."

Criterion: Matt. 7:16–17

Purpose of Christ: Matt. 1:21, John 3:16

Significance of the Word of God (i.e., The purpose of Christ is accomplished through the Word of God): Rom. 10:17; John 5:24, 3:3; 1 Pet. 1:23

Faith comes by the Word of God: Rom. 10:17

These are not all the verses employed in Part Three. We should add as much biblical information to our outline as we believe will be necessary for our presentations.

The next part of this book will examine some of the most common objections to the concept of progressive revelation, and offer suggestions for how to present this important subject to Christians.

part four:

PROGRESSIVE REVELATION

13

THE ESSENTIAL UNITY
OF THE PROPHETS

RELIGION IS PROGRESSIVE

Among the basic teachings of the Bahá'í Faith is the oneness of religion. Bahá'u'lláh writes that "manifold systems of religious belief" have "proceeded from one Source, and are rays of one Light" (*Epistle* 13). Bahá'ís believe that God has sent different Prophets, or Manifestations, at different times in history to teach humankind the knowledge of God and the prerequisites of salvation. The belief that religion (Revelation) progresses through the ages is referred to by Bahá'ís as 'progressive revelation.' That these religions appear to "differ one from another is to be attributed to the varying requirements of the ages in which they were promulgated" (*Epistle* 13).

Today, it is possible to study the development and structure of virtually all societies, whether tribal or industrial, and it is evident that religion is a universal phenomenon. According to the words of Bahá'u'lláh:

> the manifold bounties of the Lord of all beings have, at all times, through the Manifestations of His Divine Essence, encompassed the earth and all that dwell therein. (*Gleanings* 18)

Bahá'u'lláh further states that:

Not for a moment hath His grace been withheld, nor have the showers of His loving-kindness ceased to rain upon mankind. (*Gleanings* 18)

Both the Scriptures of the eastern tradition and the Scriptures of the western tradition record the successive appearances of holy men, divine Prophets, and Messengers who have brought the teachings of God. The Bible recounts the stories of many such Messengers, most notably Abraham, Moses, and Jesus. In addition to these major Prophets, other minor prophets also appeared, such as Isaiah, Micah, and so on (*Some Answered Questions* ch. 43). And, since the time of Jesus, Bahá'ís believe there have been three other Manifestations of God: Muḥammad, the Báb, and Bahá'u'lláh. The Báb writes:

God hath raised up Prophets and revealed Books as numerous as the creatures of the world, and will continue to do so to everlasting. (*Selections from the Writings of the Báb* 125)

Shoghi Effendi explained that the Bahá'í Faith regards all divinely revealed religions:

in no other light except as different stages in the eternal history and constant evolution of one religion, Divine and indivisible, of which it itself forms but an integral part. (World Order 114)

Even though most Christians acknowledge that the gradual and successive unfolding of God's plan is a fact recorded in the Bible, they commonly object to other aspects associated with the Bahá'í concept of progressive revelation. Most of these objections are related to the Bahá'í belief in the oneness of the Prophets – which they misunderstand as a demotion of Christ – and to the Bahá'í recognition of Messengers such as Buddha and Muḥammad – which they believe is not supported by the Bible.

A response to the Christian argument that progressive revelation demotes the station of Christ

Some Christians believe that the Bahá'í teachings demote Jesus, making Him only one of many Manifestations. Even though Christians can readily see that there are successive appearances of Prophets in the Bible, they recognize that Jesus is not pictured as merely one of many. Jesus appears as One greater, as a Person who is central to the Bible and to the culmination of the Bible. It is, therefore, only natural that Christians, who do not recognize any newer Manifestation from God, attribute the highest station to Jesus. Nevertheless, Bahá'ís do not demote the station of Christ by recognizing Muḥammad, the Báb, and Bahá'u'lláh as superseding Revelations. Bahá'ís believe that the Manifestations of God are, on the one hand, unique individuals and, on the other, essentially one and equal. Bahá'u'lláh writes:

> These Manifestations of God have each a twofold station. One is the station of pure abstraction and essential unity. In this respect, if thou callest them all by one name, and dost ascribe to them the same attribute, thou hast not erred from the truth. (*Kitáb-i-Íqán* 152)

When we speak of the Manifestations in the context of their divinity, none is exalted above another because there is no distinction, They are all essentially one. That is, They all speak the Word of God and guide humankind as bidden by God. If we acknowledge that Moses, Buddha, and Christ are all one, it is not possible to place one above the other. This is the "station of pure abstraction and essential unity" (*Kitáb-i-Íqán* 152).

The other station Bahá'u'lláh calls the "station of distinction" which "pertaineth to the world of creation" (*Kitáb-i-Íqán* 176). In this respect, "Each one of them is known by a different name, is characterized by a special attribute, fulfills a definite Mission, and is entrusted with a particular Revelation"

(*Kitáb-i-Íqán* 176). Thus in this sense, concerning their specific teachings, or Revelation, a distinction can be made.

In the Bahá'í writings this concept was explained with the analogy of a mirror reflecting the light of the sun (see, e.g., *Some Answered Questions* 108–9, 114, 143–5, 164, 206–7). A Manifestation of God is like a mirror. The mirror appears in various ages to reflect the light of the sun. It is always stainless and perfect, but the intensity of the sun's reflection appears to vary according to the hour of the day and time of year. We can say that each mirror is essentially the same, each perfect, none greater than another, but the light, its intensity, may appear to us to be greater at one time than at a previous time. In this way the Manifestations are all equal, yet they differ. Hence the writer of Hebrews exalts Jesus above Moses (Heb. 3:3), a point which is also made in the Qur'án (2:253), and elaborated on by Bahá'u'lláh (*Kitáb-i-Íqán* 176–9). 'Abdu'l-Bahá states:

> If in the day of Jesus Christ the Jews had forsaken imitation and investigated reality, they would assuredly have believed in and accepted Him, for the Messianic effulgence was far greater than the Mosaic. The Sun of Reality, when it appeared from the dawning point of Christ, was as the midsummer sun in brilliancy and beauty. (*Promulgation* 274)

And in another passage 'Abdu'l-Bahá states:

> Likewise, must we set aside prejudice in considering other divine Educators by investigating reality. For instance, let us take Christ. He achieved results greater than Moses. (*Promulgation* 345)[52]

With regard to His influence, as 'Abdu'l-Bahá indicates, Jesus is greater than Moses. Yet, from a Bahá'í point of view, They are also essentially equal: both perfect, both Messengers of

52. See also *Promulgation* 115.

God. Even in their teachings, where some types of distinctions can be made, They are still essentially equal, in that They both speak the word of God (*Kitáb-i-Íqán* 153–4).

The twofold station of the Manifestations can be seen in the prophetic unfolding of God's plan as outlined in the Bible. According to the Bible, Jesus Christ will return. The second appearance of Jesus will be different from the first. It signals the beginning of a long awaited peace, the establishment of God's Kingdom on earth, when "all nations" flow unto "the mountain of the LORD's house" (Isa. 2:2). In this respect, Christ's second appearance is a new and greater outpouring of God's Revelation on earth than the first. Yet Christ Himself is still the "same yesterday, today, and forever" (Heb. 13:8).

The second appearance of Christ succeeds the first, yet does not demote Christ because no separation can be made between what is essentially the same Spirit from God. This is the essential unity of the Manifestations of God. The Báb illustrates this truth by using the sun as a metaphor for the Manifestations:

> And know thou that He indeed resembleth the sun. Were the risings of the sun to continue till the end that hath no end, yet there hath not been nor ever will be more than one sun. (*Selections from the Writings of the Báb* 126)

There are times when emphasizing this station of "essential unity" in our discussions with Christians can help prevent the misunderstanding that the Bahá'í Faith demotes Christ. This is particularly true when we are first explaining the relationship between Bahá'u'lláh and Christ.

THE CHRISTIAN ARGUMENT THAT ALL THE PROPHETS EXCEPT JESUS SINNED

Christians object to this concept of the essential oneness of the Prophets because it implies that all the Manifestations of God are sinless and Christians attribute sinlessness only to Christ. Christians specifically claim that Adam, Abraham and Moses have in some way sinned. Adam is mainly remembered for His disobedience to God. Abraham appears to be guilty of at least two deceptions devised to protect Himself at the expense of others. And Moses murdered an Egyptian and was later denied entrance into the Promised Land for direct disobedience of God's command. Therefore, Christians argue, how can Bahá'ís assert that Adam, Abraham, and Moses are sinless Manifestations of God? Furthermore, Christians argue that only Jesus was free from *original sin.* We will answer these questions by examining each charge separately.

A response to the argument that Adam sinned

It is true, according to the account in Genesis, that Adam sinned by disobeying God (Gen. ch. 3). It is also true that the Qur'án and the Bahá'í Scriptures mention the *name* 'Adam' among the Manifestations sent from God. However, according to the Bahá'í teachings, the account recorded in Genesis is not a literal historical occurrence. Instead, it is symbolic and may be interpreted in many ways (*Some Answered Questions* ch. 30). It is therefore more plausible that the name Adam, when used in the Qur'án and the Bahá'í writings, is meant to signify the first Manifestation of God in a dispensation which began with Adam and culminated with Christ's return – the appearance of Bahá'u'lláh.

Even as the Bible presents Adam as the first man, the name Adam is used in Bahá'í writings to symbolize the first Manifestation at the beginning of a long period in the spiritual history of humankind. Neither the Qur'án nor the Bahá'í writings describe the life and teachings of a Manifestation known as Adam (to this writer's knowledge).[53] Therefore,

53. There are many ancient apocryphal (or pseudoepigraphical) writings and Jewish legends attributed to Adam or alleging to recount his life. In some instances similar legends are cited by Bahá'u'lláh and 'Abdu'l-Bahá,

there is no evidence to assess in order to determine guilt or sinlessness concerning the Adam who is included as one of the Manifestations in the Qur'án and the Bahá'í writings.

A response to the argument that Abraham sinned

To respond to the charges against Abraham, we must examine the Bible. According to the Bible there are two instances where Abraham referred to His wife as His sister (Gen. 12:10–20, 20: 1–18). In doing so, Abraham prevented those who were in power from killing Him so as to have His wife because she was regarded as very beautiful. Since they thought Sarah was His sister, there was no need to kill Abraham in order to have her. This protected Abraham but brought the wrath of God on Pharaoh and on Abimelech for having taken another man's wife.

Some Christians regard this as a deception (i.e., sin) on Abraham's part. Abraham did not tell Pharaoh or Abimelech that Sarah was His wife, and even when it became known, Abraham continued to state "indeed she is truly my sister" (Gen. 20:12). Shoghi Effendi offers this explanation:

Concerning the passage in the Old Testament in which Abraham is reported to have addressed His wife as His sister, the interpretation given it by some Christians cannot hold, as it implies that the Messengers of God are all sinners. A much more plausible explanation would be, that in doing so Abraham wished to emphasize the superiority of the spiritual relationship binding Him with His wife to the purely physical and material one. (*Lights of Guidance* 369)

even as both the Old Testament itself and Jesus appear to use some ancient stories for instruction. It is not always possible or essential to distinguish which of the stories or which parts are actually historical or are simply being used to illustrate a spiritual truth.

Abraham states "she is the daughter of my father, but not the daughter of my mother" (Gen. 20:12). This may mean the daughter of His Spiritual Father (God), and not the daughter of His biological mother. The wisdom of a Prophet is often misunderstood. A purely literal understanding can appear a deception if the spiritual message is not grasped. In this particular case, it is noteworthy that the verdict of God was in no way voiced against Abraham. Instead, Scripture records that it was those who sought to take Abraham's wife who were reproached by God. Bahá'ís are not alone in this understanding, for not all Christians believe these incidents are clear evidences of fault on the part of Abraham.[54]

A response to the argument that Moses sinned

Moses is believed to have sinned, according to some Christians, because He murdered an Egyptian and later, in a separate incident, it is alleged that He disobeyed God. The Bible recounts that Moses "saw an Egyptian beating a Hebrew, one of his brethren" (Exod. 2:11). Moses then "killed the Egyptian and hid him in the sand" (Exod. 2:12). "When Pharaoh heard of this matter, he sought to kill Moses. But Moses fled from the face of Pharaoh and dwelt in the land of Midian" (Exod. 2:15). Some interpret this as evidence of sin on Moses' part.

However, according to the text, Moses "went out to his brethren and looked at their burdens" (Exod. 2:11). This passage suggests the sympathy Moses must have felt for His oppressed brethren who lived as the slaves of the Egyptians. The brutality of the Egyptians may be illustrated by the rest of the passage wherein Moses is recorded as having come upon an Egyptian beating a Hebrew. The actual Hebrew word, which is translated as "beating" (NKJV) or "smiting" (KJV), can also mean slaughtering or killing, which suggests that "beating" may not convey the actual severity of the incident. Moses stepped forward at great personal risk for the

54. See *New Bible Dictionary* 8.

protection of the oppressed Hebrew slave and killed the oppressor.

It is doubtful any other recourse could have stopped the injustice. Nor is it likely that Moses could have made any appeal for His own case to the ruling Egyptians. Hence, He fled when the Pharaoh sought to kill Him. Both Moses' intervention on behalf of the Hebrew slave and His flight to the land of Midian to save Himself from Pharaoh are consistent with Moses' mission as a Prophet, for God had protected Moses from His very beginnings (Exod. 1:22, 2:1–10) and raised Him up for the deliverance of the Hebrews from their bondage.

From this point of view, Moses' motives were pure and just. In fact, the incident is symbolic of Moses' whole ministry of deliverance. Thus Moses should not be regarded as a murderer, and this incident should not be taken to indicate any sin on His part.

Nevertheless, this incident does have the appearance of murder, that is, to the Egyptians. Since this would cause the Egyptians who were attached to their traditions and way of life to reject the divinity of Moses, why did God allow this incident to occur? Moreover, why did Moses not deny His guilt, but even admit it? (*Kitáb-i-Íqán* 55, Qur'án 26:19)

Referring to Moses' actions, Bahá'u'lláh urges us to ponder in our hearts "the commotion which God stirreth up" (*Kitáb-i-Íqán* 55). He asked rhetorically, "Was not God, the omnipotent King, able to withhold the hand of Moses from murder, so that manslaughter should not be attributed unto Him, causing bewilderment and aversion among the people?" (*Kitáb-i-Íqán* 55–6). The purpose of this question is to emphasize how obvious it is that God, who had raised Moses for the divine mission, could have prevented this "murder". Instead, Bahá'u'lláh indicates that this incident was a divinely ordained test:

But inasmuch as the divine Purpose hath decreed that the true should be known from the false, and the sun from the shadow, He hath, therefore, in every season sent down upon mankind the showers of tests from His realm of glory. (*Kitáb-i-Íqán* 53)

Bahá'u'lláh says that in the time of Jesus, the virgin birth was a similar test ordained by God. Outwardly, it appeared to the disbelievers that Jesus had been born illegitimately. Therefore, to perceive the truth of Jesus' station required not judging Him by such fallible human standards. The same is also applicable to Moses.

In Egypt, the Hebrews had become a captive and degraded people. Egyptian life was valued but by comparison Hebrew life was not. For Moses to kill an Egyptian in defence of a Hebrew was, by Egyptian standards, a cruel and murderous act. Moses had been nurtured in Pharaoh's court and was living within the context of Egyptian ways, so His actions were viewed as entirely criminal. In this context, Moses acknowledged His "crime." But now that Moses had come back from Midian, God had decreed that He should no longer live according to the Egyptians. The time had now come for Him to deliver the people. The Egyptian standards and values had, in effect, been thrown down by God and Moses had come to call all those who could see the justice of what He had done. These He would deliver. In this way the pure are distinguished from the worldly and corrupt. It is easy to see the magnitude of the test for some who accepted the validity of Egyptian oppression. Who would listen to a person the people in power claimed to be a murderer? Bahá'u'lláh writes:

Were a myriad voices to be raised, no ear would listen if We said that upon a fatherless Child [Christ] hath been conferred the mission of Prophethood, or that a murderer [Moses] hath brought from the flame of the burning Bush the message of "Verily, verily, I am God!" (*Kitáb-i-Íqán* 58)

Referring to this theme, He writes in another passage:

Thus it is that outwardly such deeds and words are the fire of vengeance unto the wicked, and inwardly the waters of mercy unto the righteous. (*Kitáb-i-Íqán* 57)

The actions of Moses and the consequent accusation of murder were, therefore, ordained so that the pure in heart, those who could perceive the evidence of Moses' Prophethood, could be separated out for deliverance and distinguished from the opposers. These events were ordained so that "the true should be known from the false." (*Kitáb-i-Íqán* 53)

The second incident Christians believe is an act of disobedience on the part of Moses (and for which, they assert, Moses was denied entrance into the Promised Land) concerns the water of Meribah. The Bible states:

And the LORD spoke to Moses and Aaron in Mount Hor by the border of the land of Edom, saying: 'Aaron shall be gathered to his people, for he shall not enter the land which I have given to the children of Israel, because you rebelled against My word at the water of Meribah.' (Num. 20:23–4)

Similarly, this point is reiterated by God to Moses in Deuteronomy. Moses will see the Promised Land but not enter into it because:

you trespassed against Me among the children of Israel at the waters of Meribah Kadesh, in the Wilderness of Zin, because you did not hallow Me in the midst of the children of Israel. Yet you shall see the land before *you*, though you shall not go there, into the land which I am giving to the children of Israel. (Deut. 32:51–4)

Some Christians interpret these passages to mean that at the waters of Meribah, Moses trespassed against God by not sanctifying God among the children of Israel and, consequently, was not allowed to enter the Promised Land. But

'Abdu'l-Bahá explains that such rebukes addressed by God to
the Prophets are actually intended for the people:

> All the divine discourses containing reproof, though ap-
> parently addressed to the Prophets, in reality are directed
> to the people, through a wisdom which is absolute mercy,
> in order that the people may not be discouraged and
> disheartened. They, therefore, appear to be addressed to
> the Prophets; but though outwardly for the Prophets, they
> are in truth for the people and not for the Prophets.
> (*Some Answered Questions* 167)

'Abdu'l-Bahá further illustrates His point with the analogy of a
king. Whatever a king states is viewed as the statement of the
people he represents. 'Abdu'l-Bahá explains:

> In the same way, every Prophet is the expression of the
> whole of the people. So the promise and speech of God
> addressed to him is addressed to all. Generally the speech
> of reproach and rebuke is rather too severe for the people
> and would be heart-breaking to them. (*Some Answered
> Questions* 167)

From this point of view, the Scriptures do not indicate any
fault on Moses' part, hence no sin. Fault lies with the people of
Israel, not with the Prophet Moses. But we must examine the
account of the waters of Meribah carefully, as well as the
verses to which 'Abdu'l-Bahá calls our attention, so we can use
the Bible to convey the validity of 'Abdu'l-Bahá's explanation.

According to the Bible, Moses led the people of Israel out of
Egypt and they eventually set up camp in a place called
Rephidim. Because "*there was* no water for the people to
drink" (Exod. 17:1), the people began to criticize Moses:

> And the people thirsted there for water, and the people
> murmured against Moses, and said, "Why *is* it you have
> brought us up out of Egypt, to kill us and our children and

our livestock with thirst?" So Moses cried out to the LORD, saying, "What shall I do with this people? They are almost ready to stone me!" And the LORD said to Moses, "Go on before the people, and take with you some of the elders of Israel. Also take in your hand your rod with which you struck the river, and go. Behold, I will stand before you there on the rock in Horeb; and you shall strike the rock, and water will come out of it, that the people may drink." And Moses did so in the sight of the elders of Israel. So he called the name of the place Massah [literally: Tempted] and Meribah [literally: Contention], because of the contention of the children of Israel, and because they tempted the LORD, saying, "is the LORD among us or not?" (Exod. 17:3–7)

In this account, Moses follows the command of God, and the Bible states that it was not Moses but the children of Israel who contended against and tempted the Lord. Similarly, this scene is repeated at Kadesh:

So Moses took the rod from before the LORD as He commanded him. And Moses and Aaron gathered the congregation together before the rock; and he said to them, "Hear now, you rebels! Must we bring water for you out of this rock?" Then Moses lifted his hand and struck the rock twice with his rod; and water came out abundantly, and the congregation and their animals drank. Then the LORD spoke to Moses and Aaron, "Because you did not believe Me, to hallow Me in the eyes of the children of Israel, therefore you shall not bring this congregation into the land which I have given them." This was the water of Meribah, because the children of Israel contended with the LORD, and He was hallowed among them. (Num. 20:9–13)

Again we see that it is the children of Israel who "contended with the Lord" (Num. 20:13), whereas Moses never disbelieved, rebelled, or failed to do as God commanded Him. This is again evident in Moses' own testimony:

> Then I pleaded with the LORD at that time, saying: "O Lord God, You have begun to show Your servant Your greatness and Your mighty hand, for what god *is there* in heaven or on earth who can do *anything* like Your works and Your mighty deeds? pray, let me cross over and see the good land beyond the Jordan, those pleasant mountains, and Lebanon." But the LORD was angry with me on your account, and would not listen to me. So the Lord said to me: "Enough of that! Speak no more to Me of this matter." (Deut. 3:23–6)

Notice Moses says "the LORD was angry with me on *your account.*" Like all Prophets, Moses thus suffered for the people's sake, even bearing the chastisement which the people deserved. 'Abdu'l-Bahá explains:

> To conclude, the addresses in the form of reproach which are in the Holy Books, though apparently directed to the Prophets – that is to say, to the Manifestations of God – in reality are intended for the people. This will become evident and clear to you when you have diligently examined the Holy Books. (*Some Answered Questions* 170)

From this point of view, Moses is without sin. Some Christians incorrectly interpret the text and suggest that Moses did not believe God would bring water out of the rock because the people did not deserve it. Therefore, these Christians have come to believe Moses sinned by disobeying God.[55]

55. See *New Layman's Bible Commentary* 266.

SUMMARY

In summary, from the Bahá'í point of view, Adam, Abraham and Moses are all Manifestations of God, sanctified from sin. We have reason to believe that the Adam of Genesis is not a literal account of Adam the Manifestation, thus the accounts of Adam, Abraham, and Moses offer no evidence that any of the Manifestations sinned. Rather, those instances where sin is attributed to Them are due to the way in which people have chosen to interpret the Scriptures.

The explanations we have examined concerning these Prophets all require a careful consideration of many specific passages in the Bible. Time and circumstance do not always permit the opportunity to discuss such issues. If we present the Bahá'í concept of progressive revelation, it is therefore best that we do so in a manner that doesn't raise objections we may not have the opportunity to answer. The next chapter will examine ways of adapting our presentation of this important subject for Christian audiences.

SUGGESTIONS FOR DISCUSSING PROGRESSIVE REVELATION WITH CHRISTIANS

HOW TO ADAPT THE BAHÁ'Í CONCEPT OF PROGRESSIVE REVELATION TO CHRISTIAN AUDIENCES

When presenting the Bahá'í teachings on progressive revelation, it is important to consider what terminology will be least misunderstood by a particular audience. For example, we can say that God has sent different *Prophets* at different times in history to guide humankind. And then we can list examples, citing Adam, Noah, Abraham, Moses, Buddha, Jesus Christ, Muḥammad, the Báb, and Bahá'u'lláh. However, if we take this approach we should not be surprised if Christians react very negatively.

There are a number of objections Christians will probably raise in response to such a presentation. First, some Christians will not approve of Christ being listed as a *Prophet* among other Prophets. Second, some Christians will contend that if Buddha were a Prophet, He would have been mentioned in the Bible, and so on. For these reasons, we should not present progressive revelation in such a manner. For some audiences such a presentation is appropriate; however, for most conservative Christians it will be taken in the wrong way.

An alternative approach can be seen in the following example: "Bahá'ís believe God has always guided humankind throughout the history of the world. For example, God sent the Prophets Abraham and Moses, then Jesus Christ – the Son of God – later Muḥammad – the Prophet – and now, at the end of the age and as prophesied, He has sent the Báb and Bahá'u'lláh." This approach will also raise many questions, but by not referring to Christ as a "Prophet," much misunderstanding and many objections are avoided.

If Christians understand that Bahá'ís uphold the station of Christ in accordance with verses set forth in the Bible, they will be more inclined to proceed with questions related to determining the truths of Muḥammad, the Báb and Bahá'u'lláh. Muḥammad can be presented in the context of biblical prophecy – specifically, Revelation 11:3. This verse is a particularly good starting point because, as 'Abdu'l-Bahá indicates, it can be readily linked to the beginning of the Bahá'í era (see *Some Answered Questions*, chs. 10–11).

Our goal is, on the one hand, to avoid statements that are likely to lead to misunderstandings and, on the other, to direct the conversation to points that call attention to and support the truths of the Báb, Bahá'u'lláh, and the other Manifestations. More detailed explanations about the relationship of Christ to the other Prophets can come later, once we have established sufficient common ground.

In the last chapter it was pointed out that when we specifically discuss the relationship between Bahá'u'lláh and Christ, it is best to emphasize the station of essential unity. That is, we should not present Bahá'u'lláh in a way that implies He has superseded Christ, thus creating the false impression that we are denying the eternal sovereignty of Christ. Instead, we should emphasize that They are both the same Spirit and divine reality. As prophesied, Bahá'u'lláh is the return of the Spirit of Christ. Christians expect Christ to return, not to be superseded by another Prophet. Hence, it makes more sense to Christians if Bahá'u'lláh is presented in the context of the return of Jesus.

However, as we can see, when we discuss progressive revelation it is better to begin by emphasizing the station of distinction. Christians believe that Christ is superior to all other

Prophets and, given this point of view, they generally do not accept the Bahá'í concept of the "station of pure abstraction and essential unity" (*Kitáb-i-Íqán* 152). For this reason we should initiate our presentation of progressive revelation with the "station of distinction" (*Kitáb-i-Íqán* 176). Christians are more focused on those issues that relate to this station of distinction. Our presentation can reflect essential unity by emphasizing at a later point that it is always God's Word being revealed throughout the ages. But when we mention the Manifestations sequentially, it is better *not* to speak of them in terms expressing essential unity.

This is an extremely important point. By referring to some Manifestations as 'Prophets' and to Jesus as 'the Son of God,' our presentation illustrates progressive revelation while reflecting the terminology of the Bible and the understanding of Christians. In this way we focus on aspects of distinction that are recognizable and acceptable to Christians and which will help us avoid some of the common misunderstandings that are likely to arise.

Furthermore, it is not necessary to mention Manifestations such as Buddha immediately when talking with Christians. Buddha was sent to the people of the Far East and does not obviously fit into the succession of Messengers sent to the West. Therefore, a simplistic presentation that lists Buddha chronologically between Moses and Christ is naturally going to appear strange to most Christians. To avoid this problem, it is better to illustrate progressive revelation first using examples from the Bible and then later pointing out that, in other parts of the world, God has sent other Messengers in a similar manner. It should be noted that Bahá'u'lláh does not specifically mention any of the Far Eastern Manifestations in the *Kitáb-i-Íqán*. His audience was Muslim, so naturally Bahá'u'lláh spoke in a way that could be best understood by His audience.

The point is that we need not memorize verbatim a particular presentation of progressive revelation. Instead, there are certain things we should simply avoid saying and other things which are worth emphasizing:

- We should present Christ in a way which reflects the particular language of the Bible that is foremost in the minds of Christians. It is true that Jesus refers to Himself as a Prophet, but as we have learned, there are many different meanings given to the word *Prophet*, and Christians believe Jesus was more than a Prophet. In fact, the Bible says John the Baptist was more than a Prophet (Matt. 11:9). So it is better to use titles such as 'Son' or 'Son of God' (Mark 1:1) or 'only begotten Son' (John 3:16).

- We should avoid mentioning some details too early in our discussions, for example, references to the Manifestations Zoroaster and Buddha.

Bahá'u'lláh urges us to "teach the people with consummate wisdom" (*Tablets of Bahá'u'lláh* 16). It is reasonable to assume that this means, among other things, that sometimes it is not wise to say all that we know. And what we do say must be presented carefully. This lesson can be seen in the Gospel. Immediately after Peter recognized that Jesus was the Christ, the Gospel tells us that Jesus "charged them that they should tell no one about Him" (Mark 8:27–30). Clearly, not everyone was ready to hear the good news; other things had to be accomplished first. In the same way, once we have demonstrated the Bahá'í teachings about progressive revelation from a biblical point of view, it then becomes easier to explain other related issues.

BIBLICAL ANALOGIES FOR DEMONSTRATING THAT THE WORLD'S RELIGIONS ARE NOT IRRECONCILABLY DIFFERENT

Some Christians object to the Bahá'í concept of progressive revelation because of the diversity of beliefs that exist between the world's religions. How can the Judaic, Christian, Hindu, and Buddhist Faiths all be from the same God? How can they all teach the same spiritual truth when, in fact, the followers of these great religions are in such wide disagreement, believing many different things?

A superficial comparison of the world's religions appears to yield irreconcilable differences. The following general arguments are offered in the hope of showing that there are important reasons which can be put forward to dissuade Christians from dismissing the oneness of religion on the grounds of the apparent disagreements between religions.

The Jewish and Christian traditions offer a good case example from which to illustrate the Bahá'í view. On the one hand, Jews believe there is only one God. Christians, on the other hand, assert a doctrine known as the Trinity, a doctrine Jews adamantly reject. How can both religions be from the same God and yet teach different things? According to some Christians, God exists as three simultaneous Persons, God the Father, God the Son, and God the Holy Spirit.[56] How can God be One and also be three Persons? To some, this pluralism might appear polytheistic. However, most Christians deny they practice any form of polytheism.

Hinduism has many gods and is commonly considered a polytheistic religion. However, not all Hindus believe that the apparent plurality of gods indicates polytheism. The great Hindu philosopher Rammahan Roy (1772–1833), for example, argued forcefully from Hindu Scriptures, the Vedas, that God is One. Rammahan Roy believed that Hinduism had been corrupted over the passage of the centuries, but in its original form it was a rational faith – ultimately monotheistic.[57]

From certain points of view, both Christianity and Hinduism can be perceived as contrary to strict monotheism. Yet there are both Christians and Hindus who assert that their religions are essentially monotheistic. Therefore, the charge that Hinduism is false because it is polytheistic fails to take into consideration the convictions of some Hindus who assert

56. Barackman, *Practical Christian Theology* 40.
57. Quoted in *The Hindu Tradition* 282–8.

monotheism. Obviously, judging another religion is not a simple matter, since no religion is interpreted in only one way. In fact, some scholars believe that the western belief that Hinduism is one religion and that it is polytheistic are both misunderstandings.[58]

Similarly, some Christians deny that there is any divine origin in Buddhism, saying Buddha taught there is no God. But, according to existing Buddhist Scriptures, Buddha chose not to discuss the issue, wishing instead to emphasize other teachings.[59] Even though Buddha appears to have chosen to de-emphasize speculation about God, there are passages in Buddha's discourses testifying to the existence of a Creator which appear compatible with the concept of God in the Bible.[60]

Buddha's lack of emphasis does not indicate atheism or even a lack of importance. Moreover, it is presumptuous for us to judge the wisdom of Buddha's approach. This can be illustrated by a comparison to Judaism. Moses never makes any direct or specific reference to life after death but this does not mean that eternal existence is unimportant. Since the Old Testament is the Word of God – a point recognized by most Christians - it must be acknowledged that there is a wisdom in the omission of clear teachings concerning life after death. This example from the Old Testament suggests that it is not possible for us, because of our human limitations, to pass judgement on why Buddha emphasizes certain teachings and de-emphasizes others.

Comparisons between Christianity and Judaism provide persuasive arguments that religions can seemingly contradict yet be inspired by and originate from the same God. This apparent contradiction is not a result of the Scriptures but, rather, is due to varying scriptural interpretations.

Christians who reject the unity of religions on account of their apparent differences thus place themselves in a dilemma.

58. *Christianity and the World Religions* 138.
59. *The Teachings of the Compassionate Buddha* 32–6.
60. *Three Ways of Asian Wisdom* 94.

That is, Christians find themselves recognizing the Old Testament, but believing in the Trinity, the incarnation, and life after death, while Jews recognize the Old Testament but reject the Trinity and the incarnation, and some even doubt the existence of the soul after death. How can such differences exist while these two religions are from the same God? The answer to this question is the answer to all such questions.

Truth is one, even though this is not always immediately clear. Christians, Jews, Hindus, and Buddhists differ from one another as well as among themselves. Such differences do not constitute a conclusive argument against the oneness of religion. Instead, the differences can be attributed to two causes: (1) The different needs of each age (*Epistle* 13), and (2) the evolution of practices and interpretations obscuring the original teachings (see *Some Answered Questions* 166).

The truth of progressive revelation and the validity of the world's great religions are points some Christians will not find acceptable without a more detailed comparison of the world's religions. Obviously such a study, which is beyond the scope of this book, must be lengthy and involved. The purpose of this chapter is not to reconcile all the differences between different religions but simply to answer a few of the more common objections.

Let us briefly consider two major points that stand in favor of progressive revelation. First, from a theological point of view it can be argued that the attributes of God, such as God's all-embracing grace, impartiality, justice, love, and compassion, support the belief that God would and has revealed Himself to all peoples. Second, there is the fact that the Scriptures testify that a succession of Prophets and holy men have guided humankind through the ages. Such testimony can be found in both the Scriptures of the East and the West.

BIBLICAL REFERENCES

To make an outline of the biblical information in this section, record the following verses of the Bible and use a yellow marker to highlight each passage in the text. Where a large number of verses are specified, it may be best to simply highlight the most important verse and to put a yellow line along the side of the others.

Progressive Revelation, All Manifestations are Sinless:
    Defence of Abraham:
        Gen. 12:10–20, 20:1–18
    Defence of Moses:
        Exod. 2:11–15
        Exod. 1:22, 2:1–10
        Num. 20:23
        Deut. 32:51–54
        Exod. 17:1, 3–7
        Num. 20:9–13
        Deut. 3:23–26

SUGGESTED BOOKS FOR FURTHER READING

There are many books available that examine and make comparisons between the world's different religions. Some books are by scholars who are not advocates of one particular religion. Other books are by scholars who examine different religions from their own religious points of view. The following books were selected because they are particularly relevant for understanding how Christians view other religions.

Christianity and the World Religions by Hans Küng, is especially helpful for the study of comparative religion. Küng is a well-known Catholic scholar who has made great contributions to the global ecumenical movement. He is very interested in the world religions from the perspective of world peace. His book includes, among other things, a systematic list of how Muḥammad possessed the characteristics of a Prophet like the Prophets of the Old Testament. Such observations are rarely admitted, if even known, among most Christians. There is no doubt that K üng is limited by the restraints of his Christian point of view. Nevertheless, his book is at the forefront of the ecumenical discussion, and it contains many observations that can help Christians appreciate other religions.

There is a great lack of understanding in the West about Muḥammad and the Qur'án. Some of the barriers preventing Christians from appreciating the Qur'án can be removed by the information pointed out by Geoffrey Parrinder in his very readable book, *Jesus in the Qur'án*. Parrinder is Emeritus Professor of the Comparative Study of Religions at the University of London. *Avatar and Incarnation*, also by Geoffrey Parrinder, provides an interesting examination of similarities and differences between some Hindu and Christian doctrinal beliefs. The works of scholars like Hans Küng and Geoffrey Parrinder can help us gather information that supports the Bahá'í point of view.

To understand and prepare for some common Christian arguments against Bahá'í beliefs, we can turn to conservative Christian books such as *Understanding Non-Christian Religions* by Josh McDowell and Don Stewart. This book is part of a quick-reference series. It attempts to explain in a very simple manner what the major religions teach and why they are, according to the authors, incompatible with Christianity. McDowell and Stewart are popular Christian apologists who have written many books defending conservative Christian beliefs.

Another book of interest is *The Islam Debate* by Josh McDowell and John Gilchrist. Neither side advocates a position compatible with Bahá'í teachings, but such books as these can help us prepare for some of the arguments and objections we are likely to encounter.

part five:

CONCLUSION

15

SUMMARY AND CONCLUSION

A BRIEF SUMMARY

The introduction of this book pointed out that Bahá'u'lláh has instructed us to "Consort with the followers of all religions in a spirit of friendliness and fellowship" (*Tablets of Bahá'u'lláh* 22). Our goal should not be merely to answer Christian questions and explain Bahá'í beliefs, but to do so in a way that will help us establish and maintain that "spirit of friendliness and fellowship."

The surest foundation on which to build this spirit of friendliness and fellowship with Christians is the Bahá'í Faith's acceptance of the Bible as the Word of God. This acceptance is also important because the Bible is an integral part of the heritage of the Bahá'í Faith and part of the "indivisible" one religion of God (*World Order* 114). Once this spirit of friendliness is established, we can benefit from our ability to use biblical criteria in our discussions. We will also be ready to benefit from the practical information we have acquired to help us simplify our study of the Bible and reference the information we have learned.

Keep in mind also that the information provided in this book is only introductory and that we should always be open to continue the learning process as we converse with Christians. If we find ourselves in situations where a Christian is not receptive to Bahá'í teachings, it may nevertheless be another opportunity for us to inquire and to learn more about Christian beliefs and the Bible. The more we learn the better we will be able to teach the Faith in the future.

IMPORTANT POINTS THAT WILL REFINE OUR PRESENTATION SKILLS

Having evidence to support our conclusions is important if we are to make convincing arguments. Our familiarity with this evidence will also help us fortify our own faith. The more we put our faith on a solid foundation, the more confidence we will have when approaching difficult questions and challenging situations. In a letter written on his behalf, Shoghi Effendi stated:

> The Bahá'í teacher must be all confidence. Therein lies his strength and the secret of his success. Though single handed, and no matter how great the apathy of the people around you may be, you should have faith that the hosts of the Kingdom are on your side. (*Individual and Teaching* 23–4)

The knowledge and confidence acquired through our study of the Scriptures therefore have a great influence on our ability to conduct successful dialogues. In addition to these points, we need to consciously exercise wisdom and moderation. It is quite possible to have the right answers yet fail to be persuasive because we use an incorrect manner of presentation. 'Abdu'l-Bahá offers this advice:

> In accordance with the divine teachings in this glorious dispensation we should not belittle anyone and call him ignorant, saying: "You know not, but I know". Rather, we should look upon others with respect, and when attempting to explain and demonstrate, we should speak as if we

are investigating the truth, saying: "Here these things are before us. Let us investigate to determine where and in what form the truth can be found." The teacher should not consider himself as learned and others ignorant. Such a thought breedeth pride, and pride is not conducive to influence. The teacher should not see in himself any superiority; he should speak with the utmost kindliness, lowliness and humility, for such speech exerteth influence and educateth the souls. *(Selections from the Writings of 'Abdu'l-Bahá* 30)

By openly expressing our desire to examine the important facts from both sides, we present our discussion in the context of a mutual investigation and sharing of information. 'Abdu'l-Bahá wants us to "set forth clear arguments" *(Selections from the Writings of 'Abdu'l-Bahá* 268), but to avoid contention and heated arguments:

Do not argue with anyone, and be wary of disputation. Speak out the truth. If your hearer accepteth, the aim is achieved. If he is obdurate, you should leave him to himself, and place your trust in God. Such is the quality of those who are firm in the Covenant. *(The Individual and Teaching* 13)

If we perceive that our arguments are not being well received, if, for instance, we are not allowed to express our point of view fully without being interrupted, then we should focus on trying to change the spirit of the discussion. This may require allowing the other person or people to speak for longer periods of time so that they can feel that everything that is relevant to their concerns has been expressed. This may take all the available time. Nevertheless, it is better to show a spirit of openness and tolerance for others' views than to argue, however important the point we would like to communicate.

By taking a real interest, by asking questions whenever possible, and by giving ample opportunity for full explanations, we can help assure others that there is depth to our beliefs. Otherwise, some Christians may think we are Bahá'ís because we have not heard or understood the reasons why they are Christians. When a Christian perceives that we have heard the Christian point of view, that person may be more inclined to hear the Bahá'í view, if for no other reason than to discover why we have remained firm in our belief. Moreover, by allowing a Christian to talk extensively, we will then have a better understanding of his or her beliefs and thus will be more prepared to respond to particular concerns.

Usually people are very easy to talk to until challenged by difficult questions and controversial issues. The inability to respond with good answers leads to frustration and can be embarrassing. These feelings can sometimes lead to anger and an unwillingness to pursue further discussion of the topic. For this and many similar reasons, 'Abdu'l-Bahá's advice to keep the context of the discussion in a spirit of mutual investigation of the truth cannot be over stressed.

If we learn the evidence for the Bahá'í Faith well, it will be easier for us to concentrate on conversing in a friendly and positive way. For example, if a particular subject appears to be causing uncomfortable feelings, instead of thinking about our next answer, it may be best to reaffirm important areas of agreement such as the Bahá'í acceptance of the Bible and belief in Christ. It is also good to end the discussion by affirming points of agreement. This may require us to relinquish the issue under consideration and change the topic. If a person is not receptive to the discussion, Bahá'u'lláh indicates that we should not let this cause us to compromise our dignified manner of presentation:

> If ye be aware of a certain truth, if ye possess a jewel, of which others are deprived, share it with them in a language of utmost kindliness and good-will. If it be accepted, if it fulfill its purpose, your object is attained. If anyone should refuse it, leave him unto himself, and beseech God to guide him. Beware lest ye deal unkindly

with him. A kindly tongue is the lodestone of the hearts of men. It is the bread of the spirit, it clotheth the words with meaning, it is the fountain of the light of wisdom and understanding. (*Gleanings* 289)

The attitude Bahá'u'lláh describes is not always easy to maintain. Our enthusiastic desire to share what is closest to our hearts can lead to impatience and over zealousness. It may help our efforts to follow Bahá'u'lláh's guidance if we keep in mind that a lack of detachment and a lack of moderation in our speech can, in fact, defeat our intentions:

Moderation is indeed highly desirable. Every person who in some degree turneth towards the truth can himself later comprehend most of what he seeketh. However, if at the outset a word is uttered beyond his capacity, he will refuse to hear it and will arise in opposition. (*Individual and Teaching* 3)

This, naturally, raises the question: How do we determine when we have reached the final capacity of our audience? There is no simple answer to this question. It must be left to each person's judgment since particular situations and individual needs differ greatly. Nevertheless, the following points may be of help:

- **First**, avoid pushing the conversation to its ultimate limits by trying to cover every issue.
- **Second**, give brief answers that are to the point and allow the listener time to think over what has been discussed.
- **Third**, if an elaborate answer is needed and requested, such as a detailed explanation of the Resurrection, provide it but then avoid moving on to other topics that are also involved. One complex issue is usually enough for one discussion. Simply offer to resume the discussion at another time.

Encounters with Christians are great opportunities to share the teachings of Bahá'u'lláh and to learn more about the Bible and the beliefs of Christians. Bahá'u'lláh indicates that the objective is not to defeat opponents in argument but to win friendship and understanding. He writes:

> They that are endued with sincerity and faithfulness should associate with all the peoples and kindreds of the earth with joy and radiance, inasmuch as consorting with people hath promoted and will continue to promote unity and concord, which in turn are conducive to the maintenance of order in the world and to the regeneration of nations. Blessed are such as hold fast to the cord of kindliness and tender mercy and are free from animosity and hatred. (*Tablets of Bahá'u'lláh* 36)

GLOSSARY OF ABBREVIATIONS

OT	Old Testament		
NT	New Testament		
KJV	King James Version		
NKJV	New King James Version		
NIV	New International Version		

Gen.	Genesis	Ps.	Psalms
Exod.	Exodus	Prov.	Proverbs
Lev.	Leviticus	Eccl.	Ecclesiastes
Num.	Numbers	S of Songs	Song of Solomon
Deut.	Deuteronomy	Isa.	Isaiah
Josh.	Joshua	Jer.	Jeremiah
Judg.	Judges	Lam.	Lamentations
Ruth	Ruth	Ezek.	Ezekiel
1 Sam.	1 Samuel	Dan.	Daniel
2 Sam.	2 Samuel	Hos.	Hosea
1 Kings	1 Kings	Joel	Joel
2 Kings	2 Kings	Amos	Amos
1 Chron.	1 Chronicles	Obad.	Obadiah
2 Chron.	2 Chronicles	Jonah	Jonah
Ezra	Ezra	Mic.	Micah
Neh.	Nehemiah	Nah.	Nahum
Esth.	Esther	Hab.	Habakkuk
Job	Job	Zeph.	Zephaniah

Hag.	Haggai	2 Thes.	2 Thessalonians
Zech.	Zechariah	1 Tim.	1 Timothy
Mal.	Malachi	2 Tim.	2 Timothy
Matt.	Matthew	Tit.	Titus
Mark	Mark	Philem.	Philemon
Luke	Luke	Heb.	Hebrews
John	John	James	James
Acts	The Acts	1 Pet.	1 Peter
Rom.	Romans	2 Pet.	2 Peter
1 Cor.	1 Corinthians	1 John	1 John
2 Cor.	2 Corinthians	2 John	2 John
Gal.	Galatians	3 John	3 John
Eph.	Ephesians	Jude	Jude
Phil.	Philippians	Rev.	Revelations
Col.	Colossians		
1 Thes.	1 Thessalonians		

BIBLIOGRAPHY

'Abdu'l-Bahá. *Paris Talks*. Addresses given by 'Abdu'l-Bahá in Paris in 1911-1912. London: Bahá'í Publishing Trust, 11th ed., 1969.

—— *The Promulgation of Universal Peace: Talks Delivered by 'Abdu'l-Bahá During His Visit to the United States and Canada in 1912*. Comp. Howard MacNutt. Wilmette, Ill.: Bahá'í Publishing Trust, 1982.

—— *The Secret of Divine Civilization*. Trans. Marzieh Gail and Ali-Kuli Khan. Wilmette, Ill.: Bahá'í Publishing Trust, 3d ed., 1975.

—— *Selections from the Writings of 'Abdu'l-Bahá*. Comp. Research Department of the Universal House of Justice, trans. Marzieh Gail and a Committee at the Bahá'í World Centre. Haifa, Israel: Bahá'í World Centre, 1982.

—— *Some Answered Questions*. Comp. and trans. Laura Clifford Barney. London: Kegan Paul, Trench, Trubner and Co. Ltd., 1908. Rev. ed. London: Bahá'í Publishing Trust, 1964.

—— *Tablets of 'Abdu'l-Bahá Abbas*. New York: Bahá'í Publishing Committee, 1909–16, 1930.

—— *Tablets of the Divine Plan*. Wilmette, Ill.: Bahá'í Publishing Trust, 1977.

—— *Will and Testament of 'Abdu'l-Bahá*. Wilmette, Ill.: Bahá'í Publishing Trust, 1944, 1971.

Abu'l-Faḍl (Gulpáygáni), Mírzá. *Letters and Essays 1886-1913*. Trans. and ed. Juan R. Cole. Los Angeles, Calif.: Kalimát Press, 1985.

—— *Miracles and Metaphors*. Trans. and ed. Juan R. Cole. Los Angeles, Calif.: Kalimát Press, 1981.

Aldwinkle, Russell F. *Jesus – A Savior or the Savior?*. Macon, Ga.: Mercer University Press, 1982.

Anderson, Charles C. *Critical Quest of Jesus*. Grand Rapids, Mich.: Wm. B. Eerdman's Publishing Co., 1969.

Báb, The. *Selections from the Writings of The Báb*. Comp. Research Department of the Universal House of Justice, trans. Habib Taherzadeh and a Committee at the Bahá'í World Centre. Haifa, Israel: Bahá'í World Centre, 1976.

Bahá'í World Faith: Selected Writings of Bahá'u'lláh and 'Abdu'l-Bahá. Comp. Horace Holley. Wilmette, Ill.: Bahá'í Publishing Committee, 1943.

Bahá'u'lláh. *Epistle to the Son of the Wolf*. Trans. Shoghi Effendi. Wilmette, Ill.: Bahá'í Publishing Trust, 1941, 3d rev. ed., 1976.

—— *Gleanings from the Writings of Bahá'u'lláh*. Trans. Shoghi Effendi. Wilmette, Ill.: Bahá'í Publishing Trust, 1939, 2d ed., 1956.

—— *The Kitáb-i-Íqán: The Book of Certitude*. Trans. Shoghi Effendi. Wilmette, Ill.: Bahá'í Publishing Trust, 1931, 3d ed., 1974.

—— *Synopsis and Codification of the Laws and Ordinances of the Kitáb-i-Aqdas*. Trans. Shoghi Effendi. Haifa, Israel: Bahá'í World Centre, 1973.

—— *Tablets of Bahá'u'lláh Revealed After the Kitáb-i-Aqdas*, Comp. Research Department of the Universal House of Justice, trans. Habib Taherzadeh and a Committee at the Bahá'í World Centre. Haifa, Israel: Bahá'í World Centre, 1978.

Balyuzi, H.M. *Bahá'u'lláh: The King of Glory*. Oxford: George Ronald, 1980.

Barackman, Floyd H. *Practical Christian Theology*. Old Tappan, N.J.: Fleming H. Revell Co., 1984.

The Bhagavad-Gita: An English Translation and Commentary.
2d ed., Oxford: Oxford University Press, 1953.

Bhagavad-Gita: As It Is. Trans. and commentary by A.C.
Bhaktivedanta Swami Prabhapada. New York: Collier
Books, 1972.

The Bhagavad-Gita: Translated and Interpreted. Trans. and
commentary by Franklin Edgerton. Cambridge, Mass.:
Harvard University Press, 1944.

The Holy Bible, New King James Version. Nashville, Tenn.:
Thomas Nelson, 1982.

Burtt, C.A. *The Teachings of the Compassionate Buddha.* New
York: The New American Library of World Literature,
1961.

The Christian Life New Testament. Outline and notes by Porter
Barrington. Nashville, Tenn.: Thomas Nelson Publishers, 1969.

Christianity and Other Religions: Selected Readings. Ed. John
Hick and Brian Hebblethwaite. Philadelphia, Pa.: For-
tress Press, 1980.

Consultation: A Compilation. Comp. Research Department of
the Universal House of Justice. Wilmette, Ill.: Bahá'í
Publishing Trust, 1980.

Contemporary Thinking About Jesus. Comp. Thomas S. Kepler.
New York: Abingdon-Cokesbury Press, 1944.

Dewick, E.D. *The Christian Attitude to Other Religions.* Cambridge: Cambridge University Press, 1953.

The Encyclopedia of Islam. Vol. 3. Ed. B. Lewis, Menage, Pellat
and Schacht. The Netherlands: Brill, 1971.

Esslemont, J.E. *Bahá'u'lláh and the New Era.* Wilmette, Ill.:
Bahá'í Publishing Trust, 1923, 5th ed., 1980.

Feiner, Johannes. *The Common Catechism: A Book of Christian
Faith.* New York: Seabury Press, 1975.

Feuerstein, George. *Introduction to the Bhagavad-Gita.*
Wheaton, Ill.: The Theosophical Publishing House,
1983.

Grant, Robert M. *A Short History of the Interpretation of the
Bible.* New York: Macmillan, 1966.

Halley, Henry H. *Halley's Bible Handbook*. Grand Rapids, Mich.: Zondervan Publishing House, 24th ed., 1965.

Harvey, Van A. *A Handbook of Theological Terms*. New York: Macmillan Publishing Co. Inc., 1964.

Hatcher, William. "The Quest for the Metaphysical Jesus." *World Order Magazine*. Wilmette, Ill.: Bahá'í Publishing Trust, Vol. 12, Summer 1978.

Henry, Carl, ed. *Basic Christian Doctrines*. Grand Rapids, Mich.: Baker Book House, 1985.

Henry, Matthew. *Matthew Henry's Commentary on the Whole Bible*. Grand Rapids, Mich.: Zondervan Publishing House, 1961.

The Hindu Tradition. Ed. Ainslie T. Embree. New York: Vintage Books, 1972.

The Hindu World: An Encyclopedic Survey of Hinduism, Vol.1. Ed. Benjamin Walker. New York: Fredrick A. Praeger Publishers, 1968.

Hordern, William E. *A Layman's Guide to Protestant Theology*. New York: Macmillan, 1978.

Hughes, Thomas Patrick. *The Dictionary of Islam*. New Delhi: Oriental Books Reprint, 1885.

The Importance of Deepening Our Knowledge and Understanding of the Faith: Excerpts from the writings of Bahá'u'lláh, 'Abdu'l-Bahá and Shoghi Effendi. Comp. Universal House of Justice. Wilmette, Ill.: Bahá'í Publishing Trust, 1983.

The Individual and Teaching: Raising the Divine Call: Excerpts from the writings of Bahá'u'lláh, 'Abdu'l-Bahá and Shoghi Effendi. Comp. Universal House of Justice. Wilmette, Ill.: Bahá'í Publishing Trust, 1977.

The Jewish Encyclopedia. Vols. 1 and 6. Ed. Isidore Singer. New York and London: Funk and Wagnalls, 1904.

The Koran. Trans. George Sale, 1734. London: Frederick Warne. (For alternative trans. see also "Qur'án.")

Küng, Hans. *Christianity and the World Religions*. New York: Doubleday, 1986.

Lights of Guidance: A Bahá'í Reference File. Comp. Helen Hornby. New Dehli: Bahá'í Publishing Trust, 1983.

McDowell, Josh. *More Evidence That Demands a Verdict.* Arrowhead Springs, San Bernardino, Calif.: Campus Crusade for Christ International, 1975.

McDowell, Josh, and John Gilchrist. *The Islam Debate.* San Bernardino, Calif.: Here's Life Publishers, 1983.

McDowell, Josh, and Don Stewart. *Answers to Tough Questions.* San Bernardino, Calif.: Here's Life Publishers, 1980.

—— *Understanding Non-Christian Religions.* San Bernardino, Calif.: Here's Life Publishers, 1982.

McLean, Jack. "The Deification of Jesus." *World Order Magazine.* Wilmette, Ill.: Bahá'í Publishing Trust, Vol. 14, nos. 3 and 4, 1980.

Nabíl-i-A'zam (Muḥammad-i-Zarandí). *The Dawn-Breakers: Nabíl's Narrative of the Early Days of the Bahá'í Revelation.* Trans. Shoghi Effendi. Wilmette, Ill.: Bahá'í Publishing Trust, 1974.

New Bible Dictionary. Wheaton, Ill.: Tyndale House Publishers, 2d ed., 1982.

The New Layman's Bible Commentary in One Volume. Ed. G.C.D. Howley, F.F. Bruce, and H.L. Ellison. Grand Rapids, Mich.: Zondervan Publishing House, 1979.

Parrinder, Geoffrey. *Avatar and Incarnation.* New York: Oxford University Press, 1982.

—— *Jesus in the Qur'án.* New York: Oxford University Press, 1977.

The Path of the Buddha: Buddhism Interpreted by a Buddhist. Ed. Kenneth W. Morgan. New York: The Ronald Press, 1956.

Pelikan, Jaroslav. *The Spirit of Eastern Christendom,* Vol. 2, Chicago: University of Chicago Press, 1974.

Peter, James, *Finding the Historical Jesus.* New York: Harper and Row, 1965.

The Holy Qur'án. Trans. and commentary by A. Yusuf Ali. American Trust Publications for the Muslim Student's Association, 2nd ed., 1977. (For alternative trans., see also "Koran.")

Ross, Nancy Wilson. *Three Ways of Asian Wisdom*. New York: Simon and Schuster, 1966.

Schaefer, Udo. *The Light Shineth in Darkness*. Oxford: George Ronald, 1977.

Shoghi Effendi, *The Advent of Divine Justice*. Wilmette, Ill.: Bahá'í Publishing Trust, 1939, 1971.

—— *Citadel of Faith, Messages to America 1947–1957*. Wilmette, Ill.: Bahá'í Publishing Trust, 1970.

—— *God Passes By*. Wilmette, Ill.: Bahá'í Publishing Trust, 1974.

—— *Letters from the Guardian to Australia and New Zealand, 1923–1957*. National Spiritual Assembly of the Bahá'ís of Australia, 1971.

—— *The Promised Day is Come*. Wilmette, Ill.: Bahá'í Publishing Trust, rev. ed., 1980.

—— *The Unfolding Destiny of the British Bahá'í Community: Messages from the Guardian of the Bahá'í Faith to the Bahá'ís of the British Isles*. London: Bahá'í Publishing Trust, 1981.

—— *The World Order of Bahá'u'lláh: Selected Letters from Shoghi Effendi*. Wilmette, Ill.: Bahá'í Publishing Trust, 2d rev. ed., 1974.

Star of the West: The Bahá'í Magazine. Vol. 3, no. 11, 27 Sept. 1912. Pub. from 1910 to 1933 from Chicago and Washington D.C. by official Bahá'í Agencies.

Stott, J.R.W. *The Epistles of John: An Introduction and Commentary*. Grand Rapids, Mich.: Wm. B. Eerdman's Publishing Co., 1964.

Strong, James. *The Exhaustive Concordance of the Bible, (King James Version)*. Nashville, Tenn.: Abingdon, 1980.

Tan, Paul Lee. *The Interpretation of Prophecy*. Ann Arbor, Mich.: Cushing-Malloy, 1979.

Torrey, R.A. *What the Bible Teaches*. Old Tappan, N.J.: Fleming H. Revell, 1933.

Unger, Merril. *Unger's Bible Dictionary*. Chicago: Moody Press, 1966.

Wolfson, Harry Austryn. *The Philosophy of the Church Fathers*, Vol. 1. Cambridge, Mass.: Harvard University Press, 1970.

World Order Magazine. Vol. 3, no. 2, (Winter 1978–79): pp. 7–8, Wilmette, Ill.: Bahá'í Publishing Trust.

Writings of the Ante-Nicene Fathers. Vol. 1. Ed. The Rev. Alexander Roberts, and James Donaldson. Grand Rapids, Mich.: William B. Eerdman's Publishing Co., 1885, 1979.

The Zondervan Topical Bible. Ed. Edward Viening. Grand Rapids, Mich.: Zondervan Publishing House, 1969.

INDEX

C

THE INNER LIMITS OF MANKIND
Ervin Laszlo
Written by a member of the prestigious Club of Rome and currently serving as the Rector of the Vienna Academy for the Study of the Future, this is a spirited and provocative examination of the values and attitudes that influence the most vital spheres of our life today.

"Describing himself as a 'humanist', he may well be one of the non-Bahá'í authorities with the greatest perception of the aims and potential of the Faith. In this book ... Laszlo draws attention to the teachings of Bahá'u'lláh and the spread of the Bahá'í Faith. Not a Bahá'í himself, he appears nonetheless to recognise in this religion one of the key forces, and great hopes, for the unity of mankind ... If this book reminds us where we are going, and what we can accomplish, it will have served a very useful purpose." – Bahá'í Journal, Great Britain

160 pp   softcover   £4.50 US$7.95
          hardcover   £8.95 US$14.95

CREATING A SUCCESSFUL FAMILY
Professor Khalil Khavari & Sue Williston Khavari, M.A.
This is one of the most exciting and comprehensive books on the family ever published for the general reader, bringing a Bahá'í perspective to this important area of social life.
   Central to the book is consultation and equality within the home. Everyday examples and clear explanations, provide easy-to-follow guidance for dealing with and preventing the problems families often encounter today. Included are highly topical discussions on:

* motherhood and the new role for fathers
* organising a non-sexist household
* bringing out the best in each member
* raising unprejudiced children
* parenting teenagers ... and many more

288 pp   softcover   £6.50 US$ 11.95
          hardcover   £10.50 US$18.95

A STUDY OF BAHÁ'U'LLÁH'S TABLET TO THE CHRISTIANS

Michael Sours

This unique study of The Tablet to the Christians (Law/-i-Aqdas) offers readers, both Christian and Bahá'í, an in-depth examination of one of Bahá'u'lláh's last and most important tablets. The 'Most Holy Tablet' is primarily concerned with His challenge to Christians to recognise His messianic claims and the spiritual significance of His Cause; this commentary is thus an invaluable aid to all those seeking to deepen their understanding of the relationship between Bahá'u'lláh's teachings and the Bible.

* Fluent, easy-to-read style
* Verse by verse study of each of Bahá'u'lláh's statements
* Provides background information on many biblical topics
* Offers answers to some of the most common questions asked by Christians

240 pp   softcover £7.95 US$13.95
          hardcover £12.95 US$22.95

SCIENCE AND RELIGION

Towards the Restoration of an Ancient Harmony

Anjam Khursheed

This fascinating book, written for the general reader, addresses both a fundamental tenet of the Bahá'í Faith and a major philosophical issue of our time. As a research physicist and lecturer at Edinburgh University, Dr Khursheed is well-qualified to deal authoritatively with his subject. In a carefully argued, thoroughly researched account he traces the development of the traditional conflict between science and religion in Western society, and explores the recent developments of modern physics as they relate to our understanding of the universe and human nature.

"The author has done an outstanding service in presenting root causes of the conflict between science and religion, as well as suggestions for their resolution, in a readable book."
- The Journal of Bahá'í Studies, Vol 1, No. I

144 pp   softcover £4.50 US$7.50

THE HIDDEN WORDS OF BAHÁ'U'LLÁH

Designed to the highest aesthetic standards by leading British book designer Nicholas Thirkell, this edition was selected as one of the best designed books in the world at the 1987 international exhibition of book design in Germany, and was chosen for a special 30-book, nationwide promotion on comparative religion by the British book chain Sherratt & Hughes in July 1989.

Now available in both an elegant de luxe edition with real cloth, Persian miniature cover design and oriental endpapers and an attractive softcover version. Either edition would make a superb gift for new declarants and friends and relatives of other persuasions.

112pp   softcover   £3.95 US$6.95
          cloth   £8.95 US$13.95

DRAWINGS, VERSE & BELIEF
Bernard Leach

"Bernard Leach, who died full of honours in 1979 at the age of 92, is known to many people as a potter, in his day probably the finest in Britain, certainly the one who has most valuably influenced younger generations of artist-craftsmen. His pots and ceramics still shine like a good deed in a naughty world." – Resurgence

This beautiful, cloth-bound gift edition combines the author-artist's delicate visual images and delightful verse with an impassioned profession of faith in Bahá'u'lláh, to provide a rare insight into the personality of a master craftsman with an international reputation as one of the world's greatest potters.

* This book is an ideal gift for non-Bahá'ís interested in the arts.

160 pp 82 illustrations cloth £12.95 US$19.95

ACHIEVING PEACE BY THE YEAR 2000
John Huddleston

In this fascinating book John Huddleston has integrated the key issues in *The Promise of World Peace* into a series of practicable international agreements and objectives which provide a thought-provoking and credible route to the Lesser Peace. In a clear, jargon-free style he examines the root causes of war, explores the significance of the principle of the oneness of mankind, and presents the Bahá'í view on world peace firmly within the context of current non-Bahá'í literature and the latest international developments.

"As we approach the third millennium of the Christian era, it is ironic that visionary schemes for establishing a truly comprehensive peace should come not from Christians, but from Marxist leaders such as Michail Gorbachev, and from John Huddleston, a member of the Bahá'í Faith." – BBC World Service

160 pp   softcover   £3.50 US$5.95

THE WAY TO INNER FREEDOM
A Practical Guide to Personal Development
Erik Blumenthal

In this positive and encouraging book the author provides a simple step-by-step programme of self-discovery and self-education, emphasizes the importance of adopting spiritual goals and striving to overcome egotism, and demonstrates the role religion plays in helping us to develop our inner potential, self-confidence and sense of purpose in life. Throughout he uses quotations from the Writings to focus his arguments, and discusses many of the teachings of our Faith which bear on individual values and behaviour.

144 pp   softcover   £4.50 US$7.50

TO UNDERSTAND AND BE UNDERSTOOD
A Practical Guide to Successful Relationships
Erik Blumenthal

Written in a highly readable and direct style, *To Understand and Be Understood* is an original guide to practical spirituality. Its jargon-free and easy-to-follow advice, illustrated with real life examples drawn from the author's years of professional practice, enables the reader to better understand and apply spiritual principles in everyday situations. Using quotations from the Writings to focus each section, the author demonstrates that the practical realisation of Bahá'í principles of personal conduct and mature social behaviour is both possible and within the reach of every individual.

160 pp   softcover   £4.50 US$7.50

THE PROMISE OF WORLD PEACE
The Universal House of Justice

This strikingly beautiful, large format paperback contains over one hundred stunning black and white photographs, fifty quotations from major contemporary figures, valuable statistical information, an eight-section appendix and an introduction by Peter Khan, member of the Universal House of Justice.

* A very visual and dignified introduction to the Faith and its perspective on current issues
* An excellent study tool for deepenings and Bahá'í classes, where the paragraph to a page design and supporting material assist an in-depth study of this important text.
* Ideal for presentation to dignitaries, colleagues and friends.

192 pp 120 illustrations softcover £6.95 US$10.95

THE SECRET OF THE STOLEN MANDOLIN
Barbara Larkin

This exciting tale of exploration and intrigue follows the adventures of three children who answer a mysterious call for help and find themselves on a journey to another world. As the mystery unfolds, it soon becomes clear that this is no ordinary adventure, but a strange voyage of discovery! A lively and entertaining narrative, true-to-life characters, and themes which explore prejudice, personal relationships and the purpose of life give this book enormous appeal for the 8–13 age group.

160 pp   softcover   £2.25 US$3.75

THE PRESENT AND FUTURE OF THE WORLD (PERSIAN)
Shoghi Effendi

This book represents the first translation into Persian of that important collection of the writings of Shoghi Effendi, *'Call to the Nation'* (1977), which was compiled by the Universal House of Justice using extracts drawn largely from the Guardian's World Order letters. Most of the material in this volume is available for the first time to Persian readers in the West, and covers such topical issues as world problems, future global events, the importance of peace and the Bahá'í vision of a new world order and the constructive forces required to achieve it.

96pp softcover £3.95 US$6.25

ORDER FORM

Oneworld Publications
185 Banbury Road
Oxford, OX2 7AR
England

Name ....

Address ....

....

....

Date ....

Preparing for a Bahá'í/Christian
  Dialogue:Vol.1   £8.95$15.95   ☐
To Understand & Be Understood   £4.50/$7.50   ☐
The Way to Inner Freedom   £4.50/$7.50   ☐
Creating a Successful Family   (h/c) £10.50/$18.95   ☐
                                     (s/c) £6.50/$11.95   ☐
The Inner Limits of Mankind   (h/c) £8.95/$14.95   ☐
                                     (s/c) £4.50/$7.95   ☐
Achieving Peace by the Year 2000   £3.50/$5.95   ☐
The Promise of World Peace   £6.95/$10.95   ☐
A Study of Bahá'u'lláh's Tablet (h/c) £12.95/$22.95   ☐
                                     (s/c) £7.95/$13.95   ☐
The Hidden Words   (h/c) £8.95/$13.95   ☐
                                     (s/c) £3.95/$6.95   ☐
Science & Religion   £4.50/$7.50   ☐
Drawings, Verse & Belief   £12.95/$19.95   ☐
The Secret of the Stolen Mandolin   £2.25/$3.75   ☐
Present & Future (Persian)   £3.95/$6.25   ☐

Postage & packing:
Please add 15% to all orders (min. p&p £1/$2).

Orders and payments:
Payment should accompany all orders.